Food Culture in the
Near East, Middle East, and North Africa

Recent Titles in
Food Cultures around the World

Food Culture in the
Near East, Middle East, and North Africa

PETER HEINE

Food Culture around the World

Ken Albala, Series Editor

GREENWOOD PRESS
Westport, Connecticut · London

Library of Congress Cataloging-in-Publication Data

Heine, Peter.
 Food culture in the Near East, Middle East, and north Africa / Peter Heine.
   p. cm. — (Food culture around the world, ISSN 1545–2638)
 Includes bibliographical references and index.
 ISBN 0–313–32956–7 (hardback : alk. paper)
 1. Food habits—Middle East. 2. Food habits—Africa, North. 3. Food preferences—
Middle East. 4. Food preferences—Africa, North. 5. Food—Religious aspects. 6. Middle
East—Social life and customs. 7. Africa, North—Social life and customs. I. Title.
II. Series.
GT2853.M628H45 2004
394.1'2'0956—dc22   2004021838

British Library Cataloguing in Publication Data is available.

Library of Congress Catalog Card Number: 2004021838
ISBN: 0–313–32956–7
ISSN: 1545–2638

First published in 2004

Greenwood Press, 88 Post Road West, Westport, CT 06881
An imprint of Greenwood Publishing Group, Inc.
www.greenwood.com

Printed in the United States of America

The paper used in this book complies with the
Permanent Paper Standard issued by the National
Information Standards Organization (Z39.48–1984).

10 9 8 7 6 5 4 3 2 1

Illustrations by J. Susan Cole Stone.

The publisher has done its best to make sure the instructions and/or recipes in this book
are correct. However, users should apply judgment and experience when preparing recipes, especially parents and teachers working with young people. The publisher accepts no
responsibility for the outcome of any recipe included in this volume.

Contents

The Middle East and North Africa map appears on page 184

Series Foreword

The appearance of the Food Culture around the World series marks a definitive stage in the maturation of Food Studies as a discipline to reach a wider audience of students, general readers, and foodies alike. In comprehensive interdisciplinary reference volumes, each on the food culture of a country or region for which information is most in demand, a remarkable team of experts from around the world offers a deeper understanding and appreciation of the role of food in shaping human culture for a whole new generation. I am honored to have been associated with this project as series editor.

Each volume follows a series format, with a chronology of food-related dates and narrative chapters entitled Introduction, Historical Overview, Major Foods and Ingredients, Cooking, Typical Meals, Eating Out, Special Occasions, and Diet and Health. Each also includes a glossary, bibliography, resource guide, and illustrations.

Finding or growing food has of course been the major preoccupation of our species throughout history, but how various peoples around the world learn to exploit their natural resources, come to esteem or shun specific foods and develop unique cuisines reveals much more about what it is to be human. There is perhaps no better way to understand a culture, its values, preoccupations and fears, than by examining its attitudes toward food. Food provides the daily sustenance around which families and communities bond. It provides the material basis for rituals through which people celebrate the passage of life stages and their connection to divinity.

Food preferences also serve to separate individuals and groups from each other, and as one of the most powerful factors in the construction of identity, we physically, emotionally, and spiritually become what we eat.

By studying the foodways of people different from ourselves we also grow to understand and tolerate the rich diversity of practices around the world. What seems strange or frightening among other people becomes perfectly rational when set in context. It is my hope that readers will gain from these volumes not only an aesthetic appreciation for the glories of the many culinary traditions described, but also ultimately a more profound respect for the peoples who devised them. Whether it is eating New Year's dumplings in China, folding tamales with friends in Mexico, or going out to a famous Michelin-starred restaurant in France, understanding these food traditions helps us to understand the people themselves.

As globalization proceeds apace in the twenty-first century is it also more important than ever to preserve unique local and regional traditions. In many cases these books describe ways of eating that have already begun to disappear or have been seriously transformed by modernity. To know how and why these losses occur today also enables us to decide what traditions, whether from our own heritage or that of others, we wish to keep alive. These books are thus not only about the food and culture of peoples around the world, but also about ourselves and who we hope to be.

Ken Albala
University of the Pacific

Preface

My previous researching and writing about cooking, eating, and drinking in the Near and Middle East and North Africa mostly concerned the medieval period. Traveling in most countries of the region for more than 30 years, my wife, Ina, and I also became acquainted with the living form of this cuisine. We frequented marketplaces and hotel kitchens, private homes and cooking schools—often much to the astonishment of the people working there, who were surprised that Westerners were interested in their cuisine and profession. We started to collect as many cookbooks on Near and Middle Eastern and North African food as possible, and tried many of the recipes. Then, two years ago, Ken Albala asked me to write about modern foodways in the Near and Middle East and North Africa. My positive response to that offer was quick, although this is the first book I have written in English, and it was Wendi Schnaufer who was always encouraging me in that difficult task and giving advice. To both of them, a very warm thank you. Many questions that arose during the process of writing could not be answered by sitting at the PC or thumbing through cookbooks. As I could not travel to the region recently, I had to rely on many friends who answered my questions with great patience. Most important among them were Mona Abaza, Anke Bentzin, Bert Fragner, Gudrun Harrer, Riem Spielhaus, and Aslam Syed. Again, my wife, Ina, saw to it that I was as free as possible to write this book, and without her, the writing would not have come to an end.

Hearing or reading about the Near and Middle East and North Africa is often a sad experience. Iraq, Iran, Israel, Palestine—there is no end to the disasters. Perhaps this book presents another aspect of the region—more peaceful, fascinating in a positive way, making readers curious about the ways people live. At least, that is what I wish for.

Note: Most of the recipes provided here are found in all Near and Middle Eastern and North African cuisines. Regional specialties are indicated. The quantities, especially of the herbs and spices, are only approximate. The same goes for cooking time.

Timeline

ca. 570	Birth of Muhammad, the future Prophet of Islam, in Mekka (Mecca).
622	Emigration of Muhammad and his followers from Mekka to Medina; expansion of the first Muslim state; beginning of the Muslim chronology.
632	Death of Muhammad; end of the revelation of the Quran, Islam's holy book.
632–732	Military expansion of the Muslim state all over the Near and Middle East, North Africa, and Spain.
750–1258	Abbasid dynasty in the Near and Middle East; so-called golden age of Islam; green revolution; development of a great cuisine from Arab, Iranian, Turkish, and Mediterranean elements; first Arab cookbooks appear.
1096–1291	Seven Christian crusades in the Near and Middle East and North Africa have consequences for cooking and alimentation by importation of plants and cooking techniques from Europe.
1281–1924	Ottoman Empire; development of a court cuisine with a strong impact on cooking practices all over the Ottoman lands from the Balkans to North Africa.
1536	Ottoman armies conquer Yemen, from where coffee is now spread all over the world.

1798   Expedition of Napoleon Bonaparte to Egypt; beginning of the
            modern European colonial expansion with various cultural and
            culinary changes; importation of American plants such as tomato
            and potato.

ca. 1950   Near and Middle Eastern and North African cuisine comes under
            French and Italian influence; beginning of importation and local
            production of tinned and deep frozen food.

mid-1970s   Beginning of national emancipation of Near and Middle Eastern
            and North African cuisines and the reinventing of regional cook-
            ing.

1979   Islamic revolution in Iran and re-Islamization all over the Near
            and Middle East and North Africa, with consequences for con-
            sumer food habits.

ca. 1990   International fast-food chains arrive in the Near and Middle East
            and North Africa.

ca. 2000   Arabian, Iranian, and Turkish satellite TV broadcast culinary pro-
            grams.

1

Geographical, Historical, and Cultural Overview

THE SETTING

The cultural area of the Near and Middle East and North Africa stretches from the Atlantic Ocean to the Persian Gulf, including Iran, and from the Mediterranean Sea to the Sahara Desert and the Arab peninsula. For the production of food, it is a harsh and difficult environment. Less than 10 percent of the region receives enough rain. Even in parts of Iran with reasonable yearly precipitation, there is not enough for extensive agriculture. Approximately six different geographical and cultural regions are within the Near and Middle East and North Africa. They each form a geographic as well as a culinary cultural unit. North Africa comprises Morocco, Tunisia, and Libya. Their climate is Mediterranean in the north and hot and dry in the south and the desert regions. The next cultural area is Egypt, with the fertile Nile River valley. Egypt's climate is Mediterranean in the north and hot in the south and the desert regions. Egypt is followed eastward by the Fertile Crescent, comprising the Israeli and Palestinian territories, Syria, Lebanon, and Turkey, all influenced more or less by the Mediterranean climate and historically forming a culinary province of their own. Other areas are the valley of the Euphrates and Tigris—Mesopotamia, or Iraq—with a climate changing from the Mediterranean to the subtropical, a region with an ancient cultural and culinary heritage. The Arab peninsula forms its own cultural area and is marked by its deserts and oases. Iran, which also has an old cultural and culinary tradition, has a dry continental climate. These regions have been inhabited by humans for thousands of years. Here the monotheistic religions—Judaism, Christianity, and Islam—developed, along with their systems of sacrifices of animals and the introduction of more or less complicated food taboos. Here the first systems of writing were invented and the first complex systems of government established. One of the aims of these governments was the distribution of the precious water, needed for irrigation of the fields, and another was the storing of crops to be distributed according to different social and political criteria. From these regions we have the oldest information about various ways of cooking and preparing different kinds of alcoholic and nonalcoholic drinks. Over many hundreds of years here, humans found and tried more and new foodstuffs and learned that they could be eaten. The modern culinary cultures of the Near and Middle East and North Africa rest on these ancient traditions, although until now food historians have not taken much interest in the relations between ancient and modern foodways.

The majority of people living in the Near and Middle East and North Africa are Arabs. They have a common language. There is a distinction between the written language, which is used in all Arab countries, and many different colloquial languages, which differ from region to region and often within one region. Children have to learn this written (or "modern standard") Arabic in school. Most Arabs today are settled and live in urban areas. Only about two percent of them today are nomads. Arabs traditionally have a patrilineal social organization with strong family ties. Nevertheless, there are many differences between Arabs of Morocco and Oman in their general ways of behavior and also in their cooking traditions and modern culinary practices.

Other major groups include the Turks, who live mainly in Asia Minor—a settled people with a rich culinary tradition. The Persians inhabit a vast region east of the Arab world. Iran has different climatic areas, from the shores of the Indian Ocean over deserts to mountainous regions, so that the country also has distinct culinary provinces.

Apart from these dominant peoples, different ethnic minorities are concentrated in other regions of the Near and Middle East and North Africa—for instance, the Berbers, living mainly in the rural and mountain areas of North Africa. Others are the Nubians in Egypt, an ancient people with a long cultural tradition, now assimilated to the Arab majority. The Kurds are another people, who inhabit a region that belongs partly to Turkey and partly to Iraq. They speak an Iranian language. Their culinary culture is still very traditional.

Apart from ethnic differences, religious differences have an impact on foodways. Most are Muslim. But Muslims are divided into Sunnis (the majority) and Shiites (the minority). In some countries, the Shiites form a majority. This is the case in Iran, where the Shiite form of Islam is the official religion of the country, and in Iraq, where about 60 percent of the population belongs to the Shia. The denominational difference between Sunnis and Shiites also has consequences for culinary practice. But one also finds Christians of different branches and Jews with their long cultural history. Both minorities have their ancient special ways of cooking, drinking, and eating that has also impacted on the Muslim majority. Some other small religious minorities, like the Mandaens or Yezidi in Iraq, also with special culinary traditions, are not covered here, because today they have nearly vanished either by assimilation with the majority or because of immigration, especially to western Europe.

Some regions of the Near and Middle East and North Africa have been under the domination of European colonial powers such as Britain and France since the beginning of the nineteenth century. The colonial politics of the French were especially marked by the trend to culturally influence the occupied countries. They changed the agricultural production in many ways and also, in some ways, the culinary practice. In the beginning these changes affected only the upper class. But since the 1960s, Western consumer practices also gained more adherents among the lower classes. Since then, cooking techniques and new techniques to preserve different kinds of food, ready-made or not, were seen. Finally, globalization also has its consequences within the culinary culture of the regions. The exchange of culinary ideas and goods from all over the world has impacted kitchens from Casablanca to Tehran. In the Near and Middle East and North Africa, the ways of eating and drinking have been influenced by climatic, economic, political, and other factors. But cultural factors are of the greatest importance, and among them especially the religious one.

THE CULTURAL AND RELIGIOUS IMPACT ON THE CULINARY CULTURE OF THE NEAR AND MIDDLE EAST AND NORTH AFRICA

As most people living in the Near and Middle East and North Africa are Muslims, the impact of this religion on the culinary traditions and practices of the majority of the people will be the main focus. Some ways in which the Jewish and Christian minorities differ from those of Muslims will be touched on. Muslims believe that there is one god and that Muhammad, who died in A.D. 632, was the last of his prophets. Muslims pray five times a day, hold a fast during the holy month of Ramadan, give alms, and visit the holy places in and around Mecca once in their life. The Quran, an Arabic text of more than 6,000 verses that Muslims believe was revealed to Muhammad, is seen by Muslims as the last message of God to humankind. This is the holy book of all Muslims. Compared with the Torah and the New Testament, the Quran gives only a few proscriptions concerning food and drink. But Muslims in the Near and Middle East, North Africa, and elsewhere nowadays follow these rules quite seriously. Generally, the Quran considers good food and drink to be blessings from God, signs of his power and his mercy toward humans. In the second sura (chapter of the Quran), verse 173, it states, "O, You believers, eat from the good things, we have provided for You and be grateful to God if it is him ye worship." At the same time, food like fruits or drinks like water or milk are also seen as proof of the perfection of God's creation, so believers are exhorted to enjoy what God has prepared for them during their life-time. After their death and the Day of Resurrection, the blessed believers will enter paradise, which is described as a beautiful garden. Among the blessings of paradise—the Quran reports—are wonderful fruit and good drink for its inhabitants.

Another fundamental religious aspect with consequences for the culi-nary culture of the Near and Middle East and North Africa is the tradi-tion of hospitality. A guest was and is sacrosanct, even if he or she is a member of a hostile tribe. In pre-Islamic times, the poets of the Arab pen-insula praised a host with their power of words and did not abstain from self-praise. In many verses we find acclamations like the following: "And many a time.... I have called for the arrows to choose a barren or bearing camel whose flesh was distributed to the poor relations of all and the guest and the poor stranger must have thought themselves / come down upon Tabâla, whose valleys are ever green."[1] This pre-Islamic principle was also stressed by the prophet Muhammad and the first believers, although the Prophet exhorted his followers not to lavish all their possessions for the glory of hospitality. Nevertheless, being a good host is an easy way to gain a good reputation in Near and Middle Eastern and North African societies, and being known as a stingy person is the easiest way to lose it. Hospitality was, first of all, a task of noblemen. So, at the courts of even the smallest *emir* (ruler) during the Middle Ages and the early modern times, it was a custom that a guest was hosted with food, drink, and a bed for three days before he even was asked what the reason for his visit was. If he had no business with the host, he was asked to leave after this time.

Today, for many traditional people, a guest is still held in high esteem. There is a saying that the visit of any guest is like a visit of the prophet Mu-hammad, so hospitality has a strong religious aspect. In addition, there are some regulations or a code of behavior that had to be followed. For example, if one is invited in and offered a drink or a snack, one has to refuse a first and a second time. Only after the third offer is one allowed to accept. Of course, the host also has to offer something three times, and it would not be polite to stop offering after the second time. But there is also another aspect of hospitality that is stressed with the Syrian proverb "Good cooking is one half of hospitality only." That means that the host should also take his or her time for an interesting conversation, some jokes, or even gossiping. The social aspects of the rules of hospitality are more important than the culinary ones.

One of the more important religious aspects concerning the culinary culture of Muslims is the rule of fasting during the holy month of Ramadan. Ramadan is the ninth month of the Muslim calendar. Because Muslims use a lunar calendar, the Muslim year is 11 days shorter than the astronomical year. That is why the month of Ramadan floats through the solar year. So the fasting can take place during winter or in the hot summertime. During Ramadan, adult Muslims of both sexes have to abstain from all food and drink and smoking during the daytime—or, more precisely, from that moment in the morning when one can distinguish between a white thread and a black thread until that moment in the evening when it becomes impossible to make that distinction. After that time, eating, drinking, and smoking are allowed.

Ramadan is the month when Muslims are especially conscious of their religion. They pray diligently and avoid everything that is forbidden by the Quran and the prophet Muhammad. From a culinary point of view, public life is very much centered on the fast. So, for example, newspapers give regular advice on the technique of fasting and breaking the fast from a medical aspect and add special recipes for the month of Ramadan. In many parts of the Islamic world, camel meat is of great importance during Ramadan, because the prophet Muhammad is reported to have said, "Nobody is of my family who does not eat the flesh of camel." As in some Muslim countries of the Near and Middle East and North Africa, camels are not found in great quantities anymore; they are imported from countries like Somalia, especially on this occasion.

Especially in the middle of the month, the men pass the night praying and contemplating in the mosque. So the wives of the family bring food to the mosque, so that the men can eat without interrupting their prayer for a longer time. In North Africa, children receive special sweets on that day. The Ramadan ends with a two-day feast, the *id al-fitr* (Feast of Breaking the Fast). Normally the children receive some toys and the whole family gets new clothes. On the occasion of this feast, a sheep is slaughtered and eaten with the whole extended family.

The second great feast of the Islamic Year is the *id al-adha* (Feast of Sacrifice). The sacrifice remembers the report of the Old Testament and the Quran about the sacrifice of Abraham, who was commanded by God to kill his son, Ishmael, in the Quranic version. When Abraham is about to obey God's command, a sheep is substituted for the son by the intervention of an angel. This feast is the highlight of the period when Muslims make the pilgrimage to the holy places in Mecca. In the valley of Minah, millions of pilgrims slaughter sheep, and all over the world Muslim families join the pilgrims in this sacrifice.

The Quran prohibits certain food and drink. Some are forbidden because they are considered unclean (*haram*). Generally, everything dirty, ugly, or disgusting is seen to be *haram*. The contact with these things is polluting. A polluted person cannot fulfill his or her religious duties, such as praying. Therefore, he or she must first take a ritual bath. The Islamic law distinguishes between a smaller and a greater pollution. The smaller pollution needs only the washing of certain parts of the body, like the face, hands, arms, feet, and so on. For the cleaning after a great pollution, one has to dive completely underwater. Traditionally, for the washing, every Muslim city has one or more public baths (*hamam*) where the necessary tub and so on are to be found.

Among stuffs that are considered unclean is blood, so no dishes with blood, such as special sausages, are eaten. Nevertheless, there is a slight difference of opinion among religious scholars concerning the consumption of blood. The blood that remains in the meat of an animal after cleansing can be eaten. In the same way, organs such as the spleen and liver can be eaten. Generally meat can only be consumed when the respective animal is slaughtered in a prescribed way. The animal must be turned in the direction of Mecca (in present day Saudi Arabia), then "In the name of God" has to be said, and then the animal is slaughtered. The carotid arteries are opened with a knife while the animal is still alive. The heartbeat expulses the blood from the corpse. This meat is considered ritually clean (*halal*). But the cook is admonished to see that there is no blood left in the meat used for cooking. This blood has to be cleaned up with water. The meat of animals that are not slaughtered in the described way is called *mayyit* (death) and is forbidden to eat. The Quran says in the second sura, verse 173, "He hath only forbidden you dead meat and blood." In modern societies, where one normally buys meat in a supermarket, it is nearly impossible to know for sure whether the meat is *halal* or not. Muslim customers trust a Muslim butcher or owner of a supermarket to ensure that the meat he sells is ritually clean, and for these items they will avoid the shops of owners with another religion or from a different Muslim branch.

The rules for killing fish or other marine life are different. Fish or any other seafood cannot be slaughtered like a goat or a cow. In accordance with a saying of the prophet Muhammad, "Its [the sea's] water is clean and its death is allowed." According to Islamic lore, Muslims had found a dead whale at the seashore. They took the meat and ate it. When they returned to Medina, they informed the Prophet about it. Muhammad said, "Eat of what God has provided for you and give us to eat from it if there is anything left." So they brought some of the whale meat to him and he ate it. Muslims are also allowed to eat locusts.

Hunting was and is one of the favored sports of Muslims and non-Muslims in the regions. In the Middle Ages, hunters used an arrow, spear, or sword, but falconry was the most distinguished kind of hunting. Only game that was hunted by a Muslim, a Jew, a Christian, or a Zoroastrian was allowed for a Muslim. If the hunter was an unbeliever, his game was forbidden for a Muslim. If the hunter had hit the animal with an arrow and had brought it down, he was advised by the scholars to search for it at once and cut its throat, like in slaughtering when the game was still alive. When it was already dead, the meat could be eaten only when some blood had left the corpse. If the animal died because of blow and all the blood remained in the body, it was forbidden. In consequence, all animals killed by traps or snares by which the animals are strangled are forbidden.

It is well known that Muslims are forbidden to eat pork or consume anything that has been produced from swine, such as gelatin, because it is also unclean. The reason for this prohibition, which can also be found in the book of Leviticus of the Old Testament, is not clear, although there are various theories. An American anthropologist has assembled some of them.[2] He shows that medical reasons, especially that of trichinosis from pork, which were put forth by medieval and modern Muslim religious authorities, are invalid, because there is no danger when the meat is fried. Furthermore, having trichinosis is uncomfortable, but not life threatening. Another argument is that in a hot climate, the production of pork is very expensive. Because pigs have no sweat glands, the heat accumulating in their bodies cannot be sweated out. So they need to cool down, especially with water, which is scarce and expensive. Pigs were known in the ancient Near and Middle East and North Africa. They were used as sacrificial animals in religious cults in Palestine, Mesopotamia, and so on. Pigs were sacrificed especially for the moon goddess. So there may also be a religious motivation for the prohibition of pork. The monotheistic cults prohibited pork to fight the practice of sacrifice to a heathen god. Be it as it may, today Muslims all over the world avoid pork at any cost. Even those who do not take their religion very seriously have an antipathy to this meat. In some Muslim countries, therefore, swine is completely unknown. There is the story of a German, living in Sanaa, the capital of Yemen, who had a small dog brought from the Himalaya mountains. Every day he used to walk the dog, and many passersby asked him about this unknown creature. He informed them that it was a dog. But every so often, he heard the people murmuring, "Perhaps it is a swine."[3]

Besides pork, the meat of some other animals is forbidden. The religious authorities forbid the meat of animals like the lion, leopard, and wolf, and of birds with claws, like the eagle, hawk, or falcon. Finally, there is discussion among Muslim scholars about whether the meat of a donkey is allowed.

The other famous prohibition in the Quran is against wine. Wine is one of the good things God has given to humans. "And from the fruit of the date-palm and the vine Ye get out wholesome drink and food. Behold, in this also is a sign for those who are wise" (16:6). Then the Quran stated, "They ask thee concerning the wine and gambling. Say: 'In them is great sin, and some profit for man. But the sin is greater than the profit'" (2:219). This is followed by the quite understandable exhortation of 4:46: "O, Ye who believe, approach not the prayer with a mind befogged, until you can understand all that ye say." The most outspoken formulations against wine are to be found in 5:93–94: "O ye who believe. Intoxicants and gambling, [dedication of] stones, and [divination by] arrows are an abomination of Satan's handiwork. Eschew such [abominations] that ye may prosper. / Satan's plan is [but] to excite enmity and hatred between you with intoxicants and gambling, and hinder you from the remembrance of God and from prayer. Will ye not then abstain?" This ambivalence toward wine in the Quran made the early Muslim jurisprudence somewhat ambiguous about this drink. They considered it to be *makrûh* (to be avoided) and not *haram* (forbidden) like pork. This critical evaluation of wine was valid from the view of the Islamic law only for Muslims and not for Jews or Christians, who used wine for their rituals. In the medieval Muslim world, where the majority of the population was Jewish and Christian, the prohibition of wine for Muslims was not easily accomplished. In the thirteenth century, most Muslim scholars voted for a judicial position that stated that what is intoxicating in greater quantities is forbidden even in small quantities.

Religious minorities, of course, were and are still allowed to drink wine and use it in their religious ceremonies. Alcohol was and is allowed for

Muslims in the context of medical treatment. Today, when many Muslim migrants are living in non-Muslim societies and have to work as waiters in places where alcohol is served, Muslim religious doctors are discussing the question of whether Muslim waiters are allowed to serve alcoholic drinks. In the actual discussion, most of the jurists of Muslim law decree that it is not forbidden for them, but that they should see that they find another job. From the Middle Ages onwards, drinking of wine had to be done secretly, because the Muslim authorities, like the supervisor of the market, punished those persons who were drinking in public with up to 50 lashes. Instead of alcohol, cannabis, like hashish, became a substitute. Others substitutes were coffee and tobacco. In Yemen, the drug of choice is *khat*. All these new intoxicants and drugs are forbidden by some hard-line Muslim scholars. Nevertheless, until the end of the 1960s, wine and other alcoholic drinks were tolerated in many Muslim countries. A well-known exemption was the fundamentalist kingdom of Saudi Arabia. Other countries, like Lebanon, Egypt, and Iraq, produced wine and stronger drinks. North African countries, like Tunisia and Algeria, produce and export wine in large quantities. Algeria is said to be the greatest producer of wine all over the world. When conservative forms of Islam gained influence in Muslim countries, the prohibition of alcoholic drinks became a general phenomenon.[4] Now, alcohol is interpreted as a typical product of Western imperialism with a function in global Western strategies to degenerate Muslim societies.

There are some other topics in Islamic law concerning food that are only of regional or local importance. Here only one more should be mentioned. Iranian mullahs (Shiite religious doctors) raised questions concerning caviar, which is an important export product of that country. There is a certain uneasiness in these discussions. For various reasons, caviar is judged to be unclean. On the other hand, the economic arguments are strong to continue with the production of caviar. So now the discussion is more or less in the academic arena.

JEWISH CUISINE

Jews play an important part in the cultural and culinary history of the Near and Middle East and North Africa. The holy book of Judaism is the Torah, the first five books of the Bible, consisting of the books of Genesis, Exodus, Leviticus, Numbers, and Deuteronomy. Jews believe in one god, who made a covenant with the Jewish people. This covenant was repeated several times. The first ones were made between God and

Abraham, his son Isaac, and his son Jacob, whose name God changed into Israel. The central concept of this covenant is the idea of the chosen people, as is said in the Bible: "The Lord has chosen you to be a people for His own possession, out of all the peoples that are on the face of the earth" (Deuteronomy 14:2). Being chosen is not connected with any privileges, but means that the Jewish people are obliged to bring God's message to the world. Part of the covenant was that God promised a country of milk and honey to the Jews, the Holy Land. The Torah reports that they took possession of it around 1200 B.C. During their history, the Jewish people had to endure an exile in Babylon, and in A.D. 70 the Jewish religious and political center, the city of Jerusalem and the Temple, was destroyed by the Romans. From that time on, Jews have lived in the Diaspora.

Before the Diaspora, Judaism was a religion that was controlled by a hereditary priesthood that organized and conducted the services in the Temple in Jerusalem. It also developed through the ethical and moral teachings of a series of prophets. After the destruction of the Temple and the dispersion of the Jews all over the world, the religious leadership passed to the rabbis, religious scholars, who were the representatives of Jewish communities everywhere. Since pre-Islamic times, Jewish communities have also been living in many parts of the Near and Middle East and North Africa. From the Muslim point of view, Jews were considered among the "Peoples of the Book." That means that the Torah was accepted by the Muslims as part of the revelation from God to humankind. Where the Torah differs from the Quran, Muslims are convinced that at these points Jews have manipulated the holy scripture. The same is thought to apply to Christians and the Evangelicals.

Normally one distinguishes between two great groups of Jews, the Sephardim and Ashkenazim. The Ashkenazim are the Jews who came to central and northern Europe, whereas the Sephardim lived in the Near and Middle East and North Africa. Most of the Sephardic Jews are quite orthodox. They believe that the Torah was revealed by God to Moses on Mount Sinai and that the interpretative process by which the holy book is interpreted is both divinely guided and authoritative. This interpretative process is called *halachah*. So no law of the Torah can be changed, even if it conflicts with modern ways of living.

During most of history, the Jewish minority has been living among Muslims peacefully. This is especially the case during the Andalusian period of Islamic history, when in Spain Muslims, Jews, and Christians formed an astonishing and admirable symbiosis. This conviviality also led to a Jewish cuisine that was very much influenced by the foodways of the Muslim majority. This does not come as a surprise, because most of the ingredients were the same. But, on the other hand, some remarkable differences are a consequence of the strict food and cooking rules of the Torah. In the Book of Leviticus, the Torah forbids the consumption of certain animals and plants. Among these are pork, rabbits, hares, mollusks, crustaceans, and fish without scales. Many learned discussions have centered on the reasons for the taboos and the debate on times.

The cooking rule with the most important consequence is that the meat and dairy products cannot be mixed together. At the feast of Pessakh (Passover), when Jews remember the exodus of the Children of Israel from Egypt, they should not eat any grain, including wheat, that can be leavened. Instead, in the Sephardic kitchen, substitutes such as ground almonds, potato flour, ground rice, and matzo meal are used.[5] The biggest taboo is against combining meat and dairy products. The consequence of this is that Jewish housewives or cooks are not allowed to use butter or butterfat for frying meat. In olive regions of the Near and Middle East and North Africa, Jews use olive oil instead of butter, and in others, like Egypt or Iraq, they use sesame oil. Both of them have a strong smell when heated. This smell was part of the negative stereotypes concerning Jews in the Near and Middle East and North Africa. The nineteenth-century British lexicographer Edward Lane, who spent some years of his life in Egypt writing his famous multivolume Arab-English lexicon, reported that the Jews were thought to have bloated complexions and sore eyes as a result of immoderate consumption of this oil.[6] Modern Iraqis said that they could smell a Jewish house from far away because of this oil: "The Jews had apparently internalized their disgrace on that score, for as soon as factories were established to produce tasteless, odourless vegetable oils, they switched immediately, that sacrificing a delicious taste to prejudice."[7]

One of the technical consequences of the rules on food in the Torah is that in each Sephardic kitchen one finds three sets of pots and dishes. All pots and other utensils of a Jewish kitchen that come in contact with food have to be ritually cleaned. The items have to be immersed in boiling water and then put under cold flowing water before use. The first set serves for the cooking and serving of meat and meat products, and a second is used for dishes with dairy products, and the third only at Passover. If one has erroneously used one set for the cooking of the wrong ingredients, a new set of pots and dishes must be purchased. The prohibition of the mixture of meat and milk products is not confined to the cooking, but also includes the consumption. One has to wait three hours after having eaten a meat dish before one can consume a dish containing dairy. Or, after eating a dish prepared with dairy, one has to wait an hour before eating meat.

Although Jewish women do not take part intensively in the public religious practices of the community, one way they strengthen their religion is with food and cooking. Prayers are integrated into any act done in connection with food and cooking. Anytime a Jewish housewife cooks or fries something she should say a prayer, praising the Lord and saying thanks for what he has given. When she is washing her hands she should mention the name of God. The same should be done when breaking the bread. A benediction is said over the wine, and during any other appropriate situation during her work she will praise the Lord.[8] Jewish housewives are forbidden to cook on the Sabbath. More precisely, 18 minutes before sunset on Friday until the following evening after dark, when three stars can be seen, working, including cooking and baking, was and still is forbidden. Therefore, three meals had to be prepared in advance: one for the Friday evening, one for the Saturday lunch, and a light meal for Saturday evening. If a hot meal is to be served on Saturday, it has to be cooked overnight between Friday and Saturday.

CHRISTIANS

Whereas Jews have generally homogenous religious beliefs and practices with only slight local and regional differences, the many Christian churches show numerous variations in dogma and consequently in their religious practices. There are Copts in Egypt and Maronites in Lebanon, different Orthodox Christians in Syria and Turkey, Assyrian Christians in Iraq, and Armenians everywhere. Their dogmatic differences in many cases center around the question of the Trinity of God that split the Christian community early in its history. This split let to variations in religious practice and in many everyday rules. This also led to differences in their foodways. The different churches, for example, have developed various days of fasting. But the definition of fasting is quite the same among all Christian groups: fasting means that during Lent no meat or animal fat may be consumed. Like Jews, Christians use olive oil or sesame oil during Lent, and since the Middle Ages, Christians have eaten fish on Friday and during Lent. In the time of the dynasty of the Abbasid caliphates, one Muslim historian deplored that fish could not be found on the market of Baghdad on Friday, because the Christians had bought it all up.

One consequence of the rules of fasting in general is the development of special Lenten recipes. For example, Armenians have a quite complicated dish called *topig* that is made of peeled chickpeas with potatoes that are cooked and mashed together. On this flattened dough, a mixture of onions, raisins, various spices, and sesame paste (tahini) is spread. Then the dough is closed over the filling and wrapped in a towel and cooked like the Austrian *servietten-knödel* in hot water. Of course, Christians generally cook and eat the general food of the region where they are living. But there are two points where they differ from the Muslim majority. The first is that they eat pork, and it is only in the shops of Christian owners that one can buy it. Generally this meat is specially produced during the colder period of the year. Today, Christians also consume imported pork products like ham. The other difference with the majority is the liberal consumption of all kinds of alcoholic drinks. So, among Christians, wine is also one ingredient in the traditional kitchen, often with desserts and sweets, but also with meat. Among the Christians especially, Armenians are famous throughout the eastern part of the Near and Middle East as distinguished cooks. They are well known for their making of pastry and the famous *bastirma*. Since the time of the medieval crusades, Near and Middle Eastern Christendom has always had closer relations with the European Christian kingdoms, like France. This also had consequences for their cooking and food. With the commercial and political expansion of European powers towards the Near and Middle East and North Africa in the late eighteenth century, Christians adopted some of the European ways of living, also concerning food, so especially French cuisine and Italian ways of cooking were taken by Christians into their culinary repertoire.

AGRICULTURE AND FOOD SOURCES

Most parts of the Near and Middle East and North Africa that came under Muslim domination in the seventh century had long-established irrigated agriculture. Regions like Mesopotamia and Egypt and parts of Syria and Iran used the great river systems for agriculture. Complicated systems of canals, irrigation works, and aqueducts allowed for fields miles from the rivers. The difference of height between the river and the fields was overcome by complicated machines. Some of them, like the one in the Syrian city of Hama, are still working. It is called *noria* and is a device for lifting water over a height of about 10 meters in a succession of revolving pots or boxes. Another device is the famous *tanbur*, or Archimedes' screw, which brings water from a deep well onto the surface. All these techniques need a large amount of human labor or the use of animals such as donkeys and camels.

Today, water is also conveyed from large alluvial water resources, which are exploited in a way that even in desert regions agriculture is possible. Egypt, Turkey, and Syria built very large systems of artificial lakes by damming up the Nile, Tigris, and Euphrates Rivers. The ecological impact of all these projects is yet to be seen. One political problem of these techniques is the fact that countries downstream from the lakes fear that the amount of water that they receive will be controlled by their neighbor. The political consequences of such a situation is obvious. So even today, when modern sophisticated devices, machines, and pumps can be used, water is the central problem for the agriculture of the Near and Middle East and North Africa. Local, regional, and central authorities organized the distribution of water in the past. Also today, this distribution is a difficult task for village leaders and other officials and high political operatives. In Near and Middle Eastern and North African villages and small cities with a central and collective water supply, trustworthy and respected persons see to it that every farmer or owner of a garden receives his or her just share. This position is highly prestigious and of some political influence. By a complicated system of canals, the water flows into different fields or gardens for an exactly defined time. Of course, there have been always quarrels between the owners and the persons responsible for the distribution of the water concerning the needed quantities—owners always suspect that they get less than their due quantity compared with others. Today, the use of electric pumps further complicates the distribution. This can lower the general groundwater level, so that it is more difficult and more expensive to bring the water to the fields in the traditional way. The individualization of the use of water leads to changes in the social structure of the village communities. The importance of the role of official distributors of water diminishes, and they have lost political and personal influence. Also, the community bond is weakening. The share of water farmers receive is not dependent on their real needs anymore, but on the capital they can invest in the capacity of their water pumps. The consequences of this development cannot be foreseen. Another problem is that in many Near and Middle Eastern and North African countries, agricultural industries have been established during the last 20 years. As they are producing large quantities of agricultural products for the world market, their need for water is much higher than that of the small farms producing for a local market or for subsistence only. So the question of water will be central in the Near and Middle East and North Africa on the local and regional as well as on the international level.

As water is scarce in many parts of the Near and Middle East and North Africa, people developed a very intensive form of agriculture. Of course, there are fields where crops like wheat or sorghum grow, but more important is horticulture. Large gardens are surrounded by walls of stones or mud often protected with thorns to deter uninvited visitors. Traditionally these walls have holes at the surface by which the water supply can enter the garden. In the garden one can often find a house or a hut, where the family of the owner or his employees spend their leisure time, especially in summer when the gardens are cooler and have some fresh air. At the same time, in this way the garden is easier protected against animals or thieves. The garden itself has a system of canals according to the needs of the owner. In the garden one can find fruit trees like date palms, fig trees, and many others. These trees give shade for vegetables and other fruits like melons growing on the ground. Another combination is that of peaches or almonds with grapes.

The expansion of the international food markets from the mid-nineteenth to beginning of the twentieth century also had consequences for the agricultural system of the Near and Middle East and North Africa. Until then, most farmers produced for their own subsistence and for a local market. Then certain cash crops were introduced. Since the beginning of the twentieth century in North Africa, especially in Tunisia and Algeria, wine was produced for the French market. Fruits such as dates from Iraq have been exported since the 1920s, and oranges and other citrus fruits from Egypt, Israel, and Lebanon since the 1950s. Export made the farmers dependent on the ups and downs of the world market. The economies of most Near and Middle Eastern and North African countries were not accustomed to this, and economic crises became commonplace for many of them. The food supply for the population was not always secure, and political problems followed.

Another problem for the agricultural sector was the industrialization of some Near and Middle Eastern and North African countries. Take the example of Iraq. Until the 1950s, Iraq was exporting rice. In the mid-1960s, the country had to import rice. The reason for this was that many peasants had left the countryside and their hard work in the rice plantations and moved to the growing (and for them, economically more attractive) oil industry. So the manpower and the knowledge to tend the rice fields and the harvesting was not longer available, and the rice cultures fell into decay.

Among the most important crops of Near and Middle Eastern and North African cuisine is hard wheat and other grains. Another agricultural product of the Near and Middle East and North Africa that was envied by Europeans during the Middle Ages and early modern times was sugar cane.[9] Among vegetables, the eggplant is the most popular species in the Near and Middle East and North Africa. Spinach was called "queen of the vegetables." Tomatoes and potatoes are imported from the Americas and only have a short history in the culinary culture of the Near and Middle East and North Africa.

Fruits are one of the main agricultural products of the Near and Middle East and North Africa. The most important of them are the many different varieties of melons. Other fruits are citrus fruits, dates, and olives. The date is a very old fruit in the Near and Middle East and North Africa, and the date tree is held in high esteem. It can be found all over the region, from Morocco to Iran. The stalks of the dates can be used as shelter or fuel. The other important tree fruit in the Near and Middle East and North Africa is the olive tree. It also has a long horticultural tradition. The fruit is very nourishing and can be conserved easily. Often olive trees and almonds are grown together, because they can survive in poor soil and the flavor of their fruit is not changed for the worse by their surrounding. Harvesting of both is very tiring, as the fruits have to be picked one by one. Machines would spoil the fruits. So it is an economically interesting product in regions where wages are not high. Another fruit growing on poor soil is grapes. They do not need much rain. So there is an old tradition of raising grapes in the Near and Middle East and North Africa. (See also chapter 2, "Ingredients.")

Livestock

Animals depend on water, as do the vegetables, but in a different way and to a different degree. In desert regions, camels can live on a minimum of water and are today raised only by nomads. In the past, about a third of the Near and Middle Eastern and North African population consisted of nomads. Now, the number is about one percent. So the number of camels raised for consumption has diminished. Sheep and goats need more water, so in less arid circumstances, sheep and goats can be raised together both by sedentary and nomadic people. Cattle need more water than sheep and goats. Therefore, they are raised only in areas where water is sufficient. Cattle are only rarely slaughtered for consumption; normally they are used as beasts of burden. In addition to draft purposes, the animals were needed for the production of milk and its derivatives. Furthermore, cattle dung was used for fuel and, of course, as fertilizer. Since the 1970s the demand for livestock has increased in the Near and Middle East and North Africa. The main reason for this development was the rapid urbanization that took place in the region since the late 1950s.

Another preferred meat is that of poultry, although for many people in the Near and Middle East and North Africa it is not understood as meat. So if one declares oneself to be vegetarian, chicken is offered instead of other kinds of meat. The raising of poultry has always been a very common agricultural task. The eggs they produce are always welcome, and their meat is cooked quickly and easily. This is possibly the most important revolution in the Near and Middle East and North Africa in the provision of animal protein, as since the late 1960s there has been an extraordinary increase in the number of poultry raised for meat and egg production.[10]

Fire

Cooking techniques depend on the way heat is provided. For the traditional Near and Middle Eastern and North African kitchen, this was a central problem. As the cooking was done on an open fire, it was preferable that the fire produce little smoke. So, first of all, the fuel had to be dry. Generally the fuel that was used was wood, but sometimes it was the dried dung of camels or cows. But there is no evidence from older sources that this dung was used in the kitchen. Wood that was said to produce nearly no smoke when burned was the wood of the olive tree, ilex tree, and palm tree. These types of wood burn very slowly and produce a deep heat. Fig-tree wood, on the other hand, was said to produce much smoke. But, in general, wood has been a scare item in the Near and Middle East and North Africa. There were stalks of many trees that could be used to light a fire, but for a longer period of cooking this was not preferable. There had been woods in the Near and Middle East and North Africa before Islamic times, but they have disappeared. For example, we know from different sources that the mountains of Lebanon were covered with cedars. Now, only a handful have survived.

Coal mines are not found in the region except in the Ferghana Valley in central Asia. Coal was exported from there to the Near and Middle East. So generally there had to be techniques developed to cook the food on a slow and deep heat. Of course, the technique to produce charcoal was known, but this was complicated and expensive. Normally the cooking was done on an open fire. The pot was put directly on the hot ashes, or on some stones that were situated over the fire. Another form was a tripod from which a pot with a hanger was hanging. This type of open fire is, of course, problematic, because most of the heat is dissipated without any effect on the food.

So from an early time on, ovens were constructed. They were often made of bricks and stones with a low conductivity. The form of the traditional oven of today is about 120 centimeters high. It is a hollow, round construction with a hole at the foot of one side for the fuel, from where the fire can be lit. On top is one big hole or a number of small ones. The one with the big hole is used for baking bread. In that case, the flat loaves are placed on the inner side of the oven with a special rounded cushion with a handle. When the bread is ready, it is removed with a clasp. In the small holes of the other kind of oven, the pots can be situated so that the heat comes into contact with their bottom. These types of ovens can still be found in villages in the countryside. At the same time, modern gas cookers, like the ones used for camping in the West, are common. In cities today, modern stoves are used. Most of the stoves are operated by gas. As a central supply of gas does not exist everywhere, trucks with gas cylinders are a common sight in the cities. They drive from house to house and exchange full cylinders for empty ones. Often one also meets young boys who transport a single cylinder with a small cart. In many kitchens one finds, in addition, a single gas burner for special dishes. (See also chapter 3, "Cooking and the Kitchen.")

NOTES

1. A. J. Arberry, *The Seven Odes: The First Chapter in Arabic Literature* (London: Macmillan, 1957), 146–47.

2. Marvin Harris, *Good to Eat: Riddles of Food and Culture* (New York: Simon and Schuster, 1985), chapter 4.

3. Personal experience.

4. See Peter Heine, *Weinstudien. Untersuchungen zu Anbau, Produktion und Konsum des Weins im arabisch-islamischen Mittelalter* (Wiesbaden: Harrassowitz, 1982).

5. Claudia Roden, "Jewish Food in the Middle East," in *Culinary Cultures of the Middle East*, ed. Sami Zubaida and Richard Tapper (London: Tauris, 1994), 155.

6. Edward William Lane, *An Account of the Manners and Customs of the Modern Egyptians: Written in Egypt during the Years 1833–1835* (London: East-West Publications, 1978).

7. Sami Zubaida, "National, Communal, and Global Dimensions in Middle Eastern Food Cultures," in *Culinary Cultures of the Middle East*, ed. Sami Zubaida and Richard Tapper (London: Tauris, 1994), 38.

8. Zette Guinaudeau-Franc, *Les secrets des cuisines en terre Marocaine* (Paris: Sochepress, 1981), 180.

9. On its history, see Sidney W. Mintz, *Sweetness and Power* (New York: Viking and Penguin, 1985).

10. Tony Allen, "Food Production in the Middle East," in *Culinary Cultures of the Middle East*, ed. Sami Zubaida and Richard Tapper (London: Tauris, 1994), 27.

2

Ingredients

Today one can buy a wide variety of international foodstuffs—fresh, frozen, or canned—in the shops of many great cities throughout the Near and Middle East and North Africa. TV commercials inform the customers about new products, just like in any other region of the world. But there are certain preferences for special kinds of food that differ from country to country. Some of them are commonly used in one region and nearly unknown in another; for instance, couscous, a grain that is used in many ways from starters to sweets in North Africa, is never used in Turkey or Iran. So one has to distinguish the regional background of various kinds of food.

GRAINS

The most important grains in the region are wheat, barley, millet, and rice. Hard wheat is the most preferred type of grain and the most expensive. Husked but unground, it is the basis for couscous in North-Africa, as well as *burgul* used in tabbouleh and *kibbeh*. It is also an important ingredient for soups, gruels, stuffings, and pastries. Its advantage compared with other types of wheat is that it can grow in drier soils. It can also be stored for a long time. Today, besides wheat, barley is grown. Depending on the water supply, the quantities of production per hectare vary from 200 kilograms to 1.5 tons. Bread made of barley or other cereals is consumed only in times of distress when, because of war or bad weather, the quantities of wheat are not sufficient.

Al-Kuskus Bi-L-Khudar (Vegetable Couscous) (North African)

- 1 lb. (500 grams) fine couscous
- 3/4 cup (150 grams) chickpeas
- 8 large tomatoes
- salt and pepper
- 1 tsp. hot chili pepper
- 1 tsp. cumin
- 1 tbsp. lemon juice

Soak the chickpeas overnight in water. Put a linen cloth into a metal strainer and pour the couscous into it. Add hot water and let the couscous drain. Skin the tomatoes. Take 4 of them, cut them into quarters, and boil them in water for 10 min. in a pot large enough to set the sieve on top. When the water with the tomatoes is boiling, place the strainer with the couscous wrapped in the cloth onto the pot and cover it. Now and then separate the couscous with a fork. Remove the sieve; puree the tomatoes in the liquid; and add the salt, pepper, hot chili pepper, cumin, lemon juice, and chickpeas. Return the sieve and let cook for another 30 min. Cut the rest of the tomatoes into pieces. Take the vegetables out of the liquid with a skimming ladle and place them with the tomato pieces into a bowl. Season the liquid if necessary and reduce it. Mix the couscous with butter and place it on a warmed plate. Then add the vegetables and a part of the liquid. Serve the rest of the liquid separately.

Another important crop is sorghum (*durra*). Sorghum originally comes from Africa, south of the Sahara, and was used in the Near and Middle East and North Africa before Islam.[1] The variety that is now grown in the Near and Middle East and North Africa has been developed in India and came to the Arab world during the Middle Ages. Like hard wheat, it also has a great ability to withstand drought and to grow on poor soils. The grain is used to make couscous, pulps, soups, and cakes. The flour of sorghum is mixed with wheat flour for cheaper bread. In some regions sorghum is used to make beer. The seeds and stalks are fed to animals.

Grains are prepared in different ways. They are ground, pounded, or crushed, depending on the product that is intended. Wheat especially is ground in different grades. Generally one can distinguish between fine and coarse types. The highest quality is a very white and fine type of flour. In the villages, flour grinding is done by women; it is hard work done with small mills made of stone. In cities, flour ground in great industrial mills can be bought in shops. Traditionally the dough for bread is prepared at home.

Breads

In many parts of the Near and Middle East and North Africa, bread is the main staple. There is a saying that a Turk eats as much bread in a day as an Englishman or American eats in a week. It is eaten with every meal, and in some languages bread is called "life" or "eating." In Turkey it is called "the food of friendship." Bread is treated with respect, kissed and held to the forehead, and rarely wasted. Therefore, the price for bread is a political price. Now and then there have been violent demonstrations when its price rose or the quantity or quality of bread was deplorable, so bread is often subsidized by the government.

The bread comes shaped in different ways and forms. The most simple one is a flat, round loaf consisting of flour, water, and yeast. In the country, every family has its own oven for baking this bread. It is an oval-shaped construction about 120 centimeters high with an opening on the top and one on one side at the ground where the fuel is put. The loaves are placed on the inner side of the heated oven, often by use of a kind of a cushion. When the bread is ready, it is taken out of the oven with an iron hook. If the person who is in charge of the baking is lazy or too slow, the loaf will become dry and fall into the fire. Another technique is to bake the bread on heated iron plates. In traditional quarters of Near and Middle Eastern and North African cities, the prepared loaves are brought to a public oven, where they are baked for a small amount of money. To distinguish the bread of different families, there are stamps and markers. Some housewives also mark the loaves with a fingerprint or two. It is said that the baker can distinguish the bread without these marks. One can also buy bread at public bakeries. The ovens of Near and Middle Eastern and North African bakeries differ in size and shape. Skilled bakers whirl the dough in the air like a pizza before slapping it into the oven.

The names of bread are as varied as their shapes and forms. In the Arab world, a flat pocket-bread is baked in small rounds of about 6 inches (15 cm) across, or in larger rounds of 8–10 inches (20–25 cm). Thin types of bread are used for layering foods or for wrapping chicken. And there is thick bread that could be combined with the thin loaves. Bread is also flavored before baking. The most common type is brushed with a mixture of olive oil and *za'tar* (see the "Personal Mixtures" section below). A type of sesame bread ring is a popular breakfast or snack bread in the streets of Turkish cities. In Syria, the dough is topped with raw onions mixed with a little ground cumin, coriander, and dried mint before baking. Bread pockets (pitas) can be filled with vegetables, minced meat, and other ingredients, like with *lahmacun*, the Anatolian meat snack. It consists of thin bread dough spread with a layer of piquant minced meat, sprinkled with fresh parsley and lemon juice, and then rolled up into a cone.

The filling of a dough is a specialty of those regions where the Ottoman cuisine had a stronger influence. *Börek* is a typical filled bread of this type. In Turkey, these are made with strips of *yufka*, an unleavened Anatolian bread, which is filled with spinach, onions, several spices, minced meat, and many other ingredients. The form of *börek* can be imagined by the name of one type, which is *cigar börek*. From *börek* comes the North African *brik*. *Briks* are made of very thin leaves of wheat dough. It should be possible to look through them. A wheat flour and water mixture is dabbed onto a hot piece of metal such as the bottom of a pot turned around and put over another pot with boiling water. The leaf has to be removed quickly when it starts to become dry. It should not become brown. Today these leaves, which are called *malsuka*, can be bought ready-made in shops with Turkish or Arab specialties.

There are also deep-frozen products on the market. These leaves are filled with various ingredients. Very famous is *brik a l'oef*, which is a nice starter. This *brik* is filled with an egg, and it is an art to fry the *brik* in hot oil so that the egg white is stable while the yolk is still fluid. Bread is also baked to a crunchy hardness and can be stored like that for a while. But normally bread is prepared fresh several times a day, generally in the morning, at noon, and in the evening. Old bread is normally not consumed, but given to the chickens.

Wheat is also used in another way. It is cracked by boiling, drying, and roughly grounding. It is called *burgul* in Arabic and *bulgur* in Turkish. *Burgul* is a staple and used in salads or for stuffings. In North Africa, couscous is the traditional way of using wheat, besides in bread. Housewives consider its preparation an art. Often, in the villages, after the harvest great quantities are prepared as a staple and all women of the village work together. A half-and-half mixture of coarse and fine semolina from hard wheat is required. The simplest way is to prepare a basin of water, a shallow dish of the mixed semolina, and a clean cloth. The palm of the hand is dampened in the basin, then laid on the semolina mixture so that some of it sticks. Then one palm is rubbed lightly against the other in a circular motion to round the grains. The grains naturally fall on the cloth. The fine particles of semolina make the coarse ones stick together. Finally the couscous is dried. Any surplus flour is sieved out. Today couscous can be bought ready-made in many shops. But, of course, traditional housewives will maintain that homemade couscous is the best.

One more product is made from wheat: *kishk*. Food historians think that it is one of the oldest types of food of the world. It is found mainly in the Fertile Crescent. Yogurt, wheat, and milk are fermented, dried, and ground into a flour-cornmeal-textured substance. It is highly nutritious, tart in flavor, and somewhat reminiscent of Romano cheese. It is used as thickener in sauces, as porridge in the morning, or in salads.

Noodles

Although the legend was that the famous traveler Marco Polo brought noodles from China to Venice, thus starting the tradition of pasta, wheat pasta was already known in the Abbasid cookbooks under the Arabic name of *rishta* or *itriyya*. It was prepared from a dough of wheat flour and water that was dried a little and than cut into small slices or into many other forms. Because of the drying process, it could be kept for a while. Traditionally, noodles were added to soups and other dishes to make them more nutritious. Somehow this technique was forgotten in Near and Middle Eastern and North African cuisine after the Middle Ages, and it was a kind of reimportation from Italy when noodles, primarily macaroni, returned to the meals of Near and Middle Eastern and North African families. Still, pasta is seen as a Western type of food, and is often found on the table of middle-class families. Although the recipes in many cases are from an Italian tradition, there are some with a typical Near and Middle Eastern and North African character, especially in combination with chickpeas and spices like *harisa* (see the "Seasonings and Spices" section later in this chapter).

Pulses

Near and Middle Eastern and North African cuisine is also famous for the use of various pulses, the dried seeds of legumes, peas, beans, and lentils, which have a long history. Some of them have been found in archaeological digs dating back to the Bronze Age. In the Old Testament, Esau sold his right of the firstborn for a dish of lentils. And if one eats one of the wonderful dishes of lentils prepared by an expert Near or Middle Eastern or North African housewife, one may ask whether Esau was as stupid as he is often described. Pulses were and are still a staple in the traditional Near and Middle Eastern and North African household. Not long ago, pulses were regarded as the food of the poor who could not afford meat. Now they are regarded unashamedly as favorites of the cuisine. Traditionally, pulses are cooked in a typical pot with a special shape. It is wide-bottomed and narrow-necked with two handles. The shape allows steam to condense on the upper sloping sides and forces flavorful vapors back into the pot. The dried pulses, which are soaked in water before cooking, need a slow cooking over low heat for many hours. Today there are high-pressure pots for a quicker cooking of pulses, but the texture and the taste will differ from those that are cooked in a traditional way. One rule is not to salt pulses until near the end of the cooking time, or the beans, peas, and some lentils will harden.

Dishes with pulses are the general food, especially in the traditional quarters of the cities. The most popular of the pulses are fava beans (brown beans), called *ful*. There are dozens of recipes with *ful*—with a mixture of different fresh legumes, garlic, tahini, eggs and minced meat, or simply tomato sauce. But there is also *ful* with *bastirma* (special Armenian sausage from beef) or with béchamel sauce. The most famous dish of this type is *ful mudammas*, typically eaten for breakfast. Another famous dish from fava beans is called *ta'miyya,* or falafel. The beans or yellow peas, onions, and bread spiced with leaves of peppermint, parsley, dill, and others are chopped very fine or passed through a mincing machine. After one hour, small balls are formed, sprinkled with sesame seeds, and fried in hot oil. These balls can now be bought ready-made, so that one only has to fry them. Of course, many people say that the traditional procedure to prepare falafel has much better results. Chickpeas are also often used. They are added to many dishes made of dark meat like lamb or beef, combined with noodles, and very often used for dips, of which the most famous is hummus. In this the cooked soft chickpeas are mashed and mixed with garlic, onions, and (very important) tahini. Hummus is one of the indispensable parts of a Near and Middle Eastern table of starters, the famous *mezze*.

Hummus Bi-Tahîna

- 8 oz. (225 grams) dried chickpeas
- 5 tbsp. tahini paste
- 3 tbsp. lemon juice
- 1 tbsp. salt
- 2 crushed cloves of garlic
- olive oil

Soak the chickpeas overnight and drain. Cover the chickpeas with cold water and simmer until they are tender. Remove the scum if necessary. Take the chickpeas while keeping some of the liquid. Let it cool down for a while. Make a puree of the chickpeas and the garlic with a fork or in a food processor. Then add tahini and lemon juice. The lemon juice will make the mixture a lighter shade.

The puree should have a creamy consistency. If it is too thick, add some of the reserved liquid (a small quantity of fresh cream or yogurt can be added). Add salt. Serve in bowls or a flat serving dish. Make a longish hollow in the center that can be filled with olive oil. To garnish, add some cooked chickpeas, parsley, or cut black olives.

Rice

Besides other grains, rice is the most common food in the Near and Middle East and North Africa, and it is regionally distributed. It is very important in Iran, Iraq, and the gulf countries. Further to the west, rice is known but is not so important. While in the eastern parts of the Near and Middle East and North Africa rice is as important as bread, from Syria to Morocco rice is used as an ingredient in different dishes, as a part of a filling of vegetables or fowl, but has no primary function of satiating. Today, in Iran or the eastern regions of the Arab world, cooking rice is seen as an art. When an American anthropologist in the 1950s left the village south of Baghdad where she had been conducting fieldwork, one of the ladies of the village bidding her farewell said that she, after all, had learned how to speak Arabic and cook rice.[2] Today, normally rice is cooked to be fluffy, never sticky, with each grain firm and separate. That means that risotto, as known from the Italian cuisine, is not accepted in the Near and Middle East and North Africa. Beside the water it is cooked in, there are many ingredients that could be added, such as melted butter, oil, stock, and some spices like saffron to give it a bright color.

VEGETABLES

Near and Middle Eastern and North African cuisine uses vegetables in many different ways. Vegetables are part of salads, added to meat dishes, eaten raw and cooked, and often filled with meat or rice. Pickles and vegetables are very popular. The methods of pickling do not vary much. The normal ingredients are white-wine vinegar and salt. The pickles are never sweet. They are prepared at home, but often produced in greater quantities by specialists who display them in colorful arrangements in special shops. One could say that Near and Middle Eastern and North African cuisine is not complete without vegetables. Near and Middle Eastern and North African housewives demand that vegetables are always very fresh and, of course, ripe. Buying them is an art. The most popular vegetables are those that can be used in different ways.

Imam Bayildi (The Imam Fainted) (Turkish)

- 2 eggplants
- 1 large onion, thinly sliced
- 3 large skinned and chopped tomatoes
- 6 chopped cloves of garlic
- 1 bunch each of parsley, dill, and basil
- 10 almonds, skinned and cut into small pieces
- 1/4 cup (60 ml) water
- 1 tbsp. sugar
- olive oil

Finely chop the garlic, parsley, dill, and basil. Cut the eggplants in half length-wise. Sprinkle with salt and leave to drain for 5 min. Rinse well and place the halves side by side, flesh side up, in a pan. Mix the garlic, herbs, onions, tomatoes, salt, and almonds with some olive oil. Place this mixture onto the flesh of the egg-plants so that it is completely covered. Mix more olive oil, water, and sugar, and add it over and around the eggplants. Cover the pan and let it cook slowly for 1–2 hours. Occasionally add oil and push the mixture into the flesh of the eggplants. At the end, the eggplants should be soft and flat, filled with the mixture, resting in a slightly caramelized flavored oil.

Artichokes

The word *artichoke* is derived from the Arabic word *kharshuf*, which shows that this vegetable has a long tradition in the Near and Middle Eastern and North African cuisine. Today they are pickled, but also filled with minced meat and cooked in an earthen pot. Artichokes are also cooked with other vegetables and meat. The Turks and North Africans have very elegant way of preparing them. There the hearts of very young artichokes are cooked gently in olive oil. Their taste is complemented with spring onions and dill, and they are eaten cold.

Asparagus

In modern Near and Middle Eastern and North African cuisine, asparagus plays a minor role and is used in the same way as in Europe.

Cabbages

Cabbage is not a popular vegetable in the Near and Middle Eastern and North African kitchen. There are only two general ways of preparing it.

It is pickled or used as an envelope for various stuffings made of minced meat, onions, nuts, and other vegetables. Cauliflower is a new type of vegetable in the regions. It is eaten pickled, but is also fried after having been dressed with eggs and bread crumbs. In another recipe, cauliflower is combined with minced meat, green peppers, and tomatoes in a kind of a soufflé.

Carrots

Carrots have always been a very popular vegetable in the Near and Middle East and North Africa. They were and still are an ingredient during wintertime and are often combined with meat. As their taste has a certain sweetness, they are found in sweet-sour combinations. In North Africa there are recipes where carrots are cooked together with fruits, mainly raisins and other dry fruit. They are also often pickled. Although carrots are a staple, they are not exported, mainly because they grow nearly everywhere, on poor ground and with low quantities of rain.

Zeytinyagli Havuc (Carrots and Lentils)

- 4 peeled and sliced carrots
- 1/2 cup (100 grams) small green lentils
- 1 onion
- 3 chopped cloves of garlic
- 1 tbsp. coriander seeds
- 4 tbsp. olive oil
- 1 tbsp. tomato puree
- 1 tsp. sugar
- 1 cup (250 ml) water
- 1 bunch each of fresh dill, parsley, and chopped mint
- salt and pepper

Soak the lentils for 2–3 hours, then drain and put into a pan, cover with fresh water, bring to a boil, and let simmer for 10–15 min. Drain well. Heat oil in a pan and add the sliced and quartered onion, the garlic, and the coriander seeds. Add the carrots and let cook for 3 min. Let the onion and garlic become soft. Stir in the lentils, tomato puree, and sugar. Add water and bring to boil. Then reduce the heat, cover, and simmer for 30 min. Add the fresh herbs, salt, and pepper, and continue to simmer uncovered for 10 min. until most of the liquid has evaporated. Leave to cool and serve.

Cucumbers

Cucumbers were popular in the medieval Near and Middle Eastern and North African kitchen. They could be found on the market year-round. Often they were combined with meat, especially lamb meat. Medieval cookbooks offer a combination of cucumbers and sour milk, so one could say that the well-known, refreshing Turkish dish *cacik*, the mixture of cucumbers and yogurt seasoned with salt, pepper, garlic, and mint, has a long history. Because of its high water content, cucumbers are very thirst quenching, and therefore are one ingredient of mixed salads. In North Africa, a good salad is made with cucumbers and pomegranate seeds.

Cacik (Yogurt and Cucumber Salad) (Turkish)

- 1 cucumber
- 1 cup (250 ml) thick yogurt
- 2–3 cloves of garlic, crushed with salt
- 1 small bunch of fresh mint leaves, finely chopped
- salt and pepper

Mix the yogurt with garlic and add salt and pepper. Chop the mint and stir it in. Cut the cucumber in small slices, add salt, and let it rest for 4 min. Then drain off the excess water. Rinse the cucumber and add it to the yogurt.

Fattûsh (Wet Bread)

- Half of a large, crispy loaf of leftover Arabic bread (or pita)
- 6 lettuce leaves
- 1 large or 2 small cucumbers and any other chopped vegetables
- 4 tbsp. chopped spring onions
- 4 tbsp. parsley
- 2 tomatoes, cubed, without the skin
- fresh lemon juice
- olive oil
- 1 clove crushed garlic
- 3 tsp. sumac
- salt and pepper

Separate the 2 layers of the Arabic bread and break it into small pieces. Wash and chop the vegetables and tear the herbs with your hands. Prepare a dressing with garlic, lemon juice, olive oil, salt, and pepper. Toss the bread, sumac and dressing into the salad.

Note: Sumac is the ground, sour, red berry of a plant that grows in the Middle East and in North America and can be bought in Middle Eastern grocery stores. It should not be confused with poison sumac, which is white.

Eggplants

Eggplants are the most popular vegetable in the Near and Middle Eastern and North African cuisine. Originally coming from India, they are sometimes referred to as the poor man's meat, which shows that they were always also very cheap. Eggplants have no strong taste themselves, but easily absorb and strengthen the flavor of those ingredients they are combined with. Therefore, they are cooked in an uncountable number of ways. Available year-round, they range from bulbous and gourdlike to long and slender. The rounder ones are good for grilling over charcoal, and the longer are used for filling. Eggplants are also dried and hung in the markets like chunky necklaces and, once reconstituted with water, can be filled with rice and cooked in olive oil. They can also be filled with whole chili peppers. They are mashed and mixed with tahini and used as part of the *mezze*. One of the most famous dishes with eggplant is Turkish and is called *imam bayildi*, which means "the imam fainted." As the story goes, the imam became unconscious with sheer pleasure at the sight of this dish, or he lost consciousness because he had eaten too much of it. For this recipe, the eggplant, onion, and tomato should be so tender and delicately intertwined that they melt in the mouth. Eggplants can be made into a soufflé in combination with minced meat, tomato, or a béchamel sauce. In the Turkish city of Antalya, a jam is even made from eggplant, which, surprisingly, tastes of bananas.

Eggplant *Musakka* (Moussaka)

- 4 eggplants, cut into slices, sprinkled with water, and left for 2 hours
- sunflower oil for frying
- 2 tbsp. olive oil
- 2 chopped onions
- 6 chopped cloves of garlic

- 2 tbsp. currants, soaked in water
- 1 lb. (500 grams) lean minced meat
- 2 tbsp. ground cinnamon
- 2 tbsp. oregano
- salt and pepper

Béchamel Sauce

- 1 tbsp. butter
- 3 tbsp. plain flour
- 1 1/4 cups (300 ml) milk
- salt
- ground nutmeg

Drain the eggplant slices and squeeze dry. Heat a thick layer of sunflower oil and fry them. Place on paper towels to drain. Heat olive oil in a pan and soften onions and garlic and the currants, add the lamb meat, and cook for 5 min. or until the liquid has been absorbed. Season with salt and pepper. Layer the eggplant and meat tightly in an oven-proof dish, starting and ending with the eggplant. Now prepare the béchamel sauce: melt butter in a saucepan, remove from the heat, and stir in enough flour to make a thick roux. Add milk and stir continuously until the sauce is thick and smooth. Season with salt and nutmeg. (Instead of the sauce, you can mix 2 beaten eggs, tomato ketchup, salt, pepper, and water and pour it over the meat and eggplant.) Spoon the sauce evenly over the eggplant, place the dish in an oven at 300 degrees, and bake until browned on top.

Garlic

Like in other countries with a Mediterranean or hot climate, garlic is often used. It is used in dry and fresh forms. It is also pickled with and without its skin. It is believed to ward off the evil eye and to contain healing effects beneficial to the circulation of the blood. The odor of garlic, however, was and is detested by many. It is reported that the prophet Muhammad did not like garlic. Ethnic prejudices often are combined with the consuming of garlic. Great quantities of garlic are used in traditional recipes. There are some with up to 20 cloves, typical for the kitchen of the countryside. The more refined cuisine of the Near and Middle East and North Africa uses only small quantities, and in specific dishes. In this cuisine, garlic is crushed to a pulp with salt, which acts as an abrasive.

Leeks

Leeks are preferably cooked in olive oil and served as an accompaniment to meat. A nice combination is that of leeks and carrots. Cooked and seasoned leeks are also used as a filling in dough and baked.

Moulikhiyya

Moulikhiyya (Jew's mallow; *Corchorus olitorius*) is a very old Near and Middle Eastern and North African vegetable coming originally from India. It stems from the linden family and resembles spinach or chard, but has the properties of okra. *Moulikhiyya* in the Middle Ages was thought to be a sexual stimulant, inducing women to have sexual contact with strangers after having eaten it. The sexual appetite of men was also wetted by *moulikhiyya*. It is a specialty of Egypt. Only the willow-leaf-like leaves are used, fresh or dried. They are cooked together with garlic and various seasonings on a fond made from chicken or lamb. The results are a soup-like consistency that is seasoned with lemon juice. A Western taste has to get accustomed to this dish. Often the vegetable is combined with meat such as chicken or lamb. The dried variant is also added to stews of meat of chicken or lamb.

Okra

Because of its softness, okra has the name "ladies' fingers" all over the Near and Middle East and North Africa. It is often cooked in combination with green beans and tomatoes. Okra is also combined with lamb meat. Turkish cuisine has an interesting recipe for a soup with dried okra. Because the soup has a special sour taste, it is often served at ceremonial feasts like marriages as a palate cleanser between the courses.

Onions

There are many different varieties of onions in the Near and Middle East and North Africa. One finds them in colors like red, purple, pink, gold, and white. There are spring onions and shallots. They all taste different; some are sweet, others are sharp. They are produced abundantly in all parts of the region. Besides their complementing other dishes, onions also stand on their own. Large white onions, for example, are stuffed with minced meat and rice.

Peppers

There are many varieties of peppers. There are sweet ones that are large red and yellow, and bell-shaped. They can be grilled and the skin removed. Dripped with some vinegar, they make a wonderful light starter. The small green bell peppers are picked unripe and used for stuffing with rice or minced meat. Like eggplant, the small red ones can be dried and saved for a time. Then they are reconstituted with water and stuffed. There are also green or red, long, twisted peppers, ranging in hotness from pleasant to uncomfortable. They are added to salads or combined with grilled meat.

Potatoes

As the potato originated in the Americas, it was introduced in the Near and Middle East and North Africa only recently. There is no exact information on how the importation came about. As in Europe, the government convinced the peasants to try this new item, so the Ottoman government paid small sums to peasants in Mesopotamia if they were willing to grow potato in the 1880s. But it took some time until potatoes were accepted in Near and Middle Eastern and North African cuisine. Only after the 1950s did cooks in the Near and Middle East and North Africa start to develop their own ways of dealing with potatoes. The first recipes of this type were combinations of fried potatoes with Near and Middle Eastern and North African seasonings like *sumakh* and types of frying fat. Then the proclivity for stuffed vegetables had its impact on potatoes. They are cooked, peeled, and filled with minced meat and onions or nuts and tomatoes and put in the oven for some time. Minced meat is also mixed into balls of mashed potatoes and fried in hot oil in a pan. There are also interesting potato casseroles where the potatoes are combined with onions, tomatoes, and black olives.

Tomatoes

As the tomato, like the potato, comes from the Americas, it also has a short history in Near and Middle Eastern and North African cuisine. Tomatoes were imported into the Ottoman Empire in the seventeenth century and spread from Istanbul to many of its provinces. Tomatoes are now one of the main food exports of many Near and Middle Eastern and North African countries. They come tinned whole or chopped, dried, and pressed into a thick paste or puree. In season, one can find them piled up in rural markets. Among other things, tomatoes have one important advantage: if they are sprinkled with water by the farmer on the way to the market or at the market itself to keep them looking fresh, they will have dots that detract from their appearance. The water is often polluted and causes digestive problems. Farmers refrain from sprinkling tomatoes for optical reasons. One of the first rules for a visitor concerning food is "Never eat green salad, but you can eat tomatoes."

With tomatoes, especially in dried form, one can improve the taste of many Near and Middle Eastern and North African dishes. Drying tomatoes are to be found in the late summer on many of the flat roofs of the countryside in many Near and Middle Eastern and North African villages. For home cooking, they are cut into slices of 5 millimeters each, placed lightly on a wire mesh, and put out under the sun. If they are dry on one side, they have to be turned over on the other side and salted again. At night, they have to be taken indoors to avoid humidity. After two to three days, the tomato slices feel like soft leather. The dried tomato slices are packed into plastic bags and can be stored for six months. The dried tomatoes are worked into a thick paste and used like ketchup. Tomatoes are used in many different forms, but the most important is surely to give its slightly sour taste to many dishes. Therefore, one finds them in combination with meat, fish, and various vegetables.

Lubia Bi-L-Banadura (Green Beans and Tomatoes)

- 1 lb. (500 grams) green beans
- 1 sliced onion
- 4 chopped cloves of garlic
- 4 tbsp. olive oil
- 2 skinned and roughly chopped tomatoes
- 1 tsp. sugar
- lemon juice
- salt and pepper
- water

Heat olive oil and soften onion and garlic in it. Add the tomatoes and sugar and let cook for 3 min. Add the beans and cover with water. Bring the liquid to boil, reduce the heat, cover, and let simmer for 30 min. Add lemon juice, salt, and pepper, and let simmer uncovered for 15 min. until most of the liquid has evaporated, then serve.

Spinach

Spinach has a long history in Near and Middle Eastern and North African cuisine. In some recipes, spinach was combined with peppermint in equal quantities. Also, for aesthetic effect, spinach was combined with eggs. In modern cuisine, spinach is used in salads and in soups, often in combination with meat, and in North Africa also with dried plums. Today frozen spinach is also used.

Zucchinis

Like eggplant, zucchini is a very popular vegetable because of the many ways in which it can be cooked. One can fry slices of zucchini spiced or combined with egg white and flour in oil. There are recipes for frying them after having beaten eggs mixed with flour, salt and pepper, mint, and parsley, combined with squashed zucchinis, and formed into small balls in hot oil. But the most spectacular way of preparing them is by stuffing. A zucchini is reamed from one side lengthwise and stuffed with mixtures of meat and/or onions, dried spearmint, and pine nuts. An easier technique is to cut zucchinis in half lengthwise, hollow them out, and fill them with the mixture. Zucchini can also be pickled, which makes for good starters and is a way of conserving this vegetable for a time.

MUSHROOMS AND TRUFFLES

Mushrooms are rare in the Near and Middle East and North Africa. They are found only in regions with sufficient quantities of annual rain, like the mountain areas in Anatolia, so recipes with mushrooms are very rare in cookbooks. In Turkey they are cooked in olive oil and butter with garlic and various spices, then tossed in a blend of fresh herbs. Traditionally, truffles are better known. A variety of truffles can be found on the common markets of the Near and Middle East and North Africa. So-called desert truffles found in Kuwait and Iraq are said to have nearly no smell or taste, and it is nearly impossible to clean them of sand. White desert truffles of Saudi Arabia are more tasty and, if on the market, are often used instead of meat. In Turkey, truffles are roasted together with minced meat on skewers, and taste and smell like almonds. There are also reports of truffles in Morocco and Tunisia that taste like potatoes.

GRAPE LEAVES

Grape leaves are commonly used in all cuisines of the Near and Middle East and North Africa, but they are a more modern ingredient because they are not mentioned in medieval Near Eastern cookbooks. The grape leaves are used primarily with different fillings. The fresh leaves are bought in the market when the leaves are still young. Old leaves are also used, but the younger ones are preferred when used immediately. The older ones are good if they are preserved. Today they can even be bought frozen. But the normal method of preservation is by putting them in salted water or a brine plus an additional saltwater solution in a crock.

Grape leaves are stuffed with different fillings like seasoned rice or minced meat. The ones with a rice filling can also be bought ready-made in canned form. But, of course, everybody will swear that homemade ones are much better. Stuffed vine leaves are served as starters and are an indispensable part of every *mezze*. But there are other ways of using grape leaves. Small and medium-sized fish can be wrapped in grape leaves and then be poached or grilled. They add a tasty smell to the fish. For bigger fish such as trout, swordfish, tuna, or shark, small chunks are cut, wrapped in grape leaves, and grilled on a kebab stick or spear. Different kinds of cheese also can be wrapped into grape leaves and eaten raw or grilled. And in Turkey, a pie from grape leaves and yogurt is seasoned with dill and mint.

Yaprak Dolmasi (Stuffed Grape Leaves Vegetarian Version)

- 8 oz. (225 grams) grape leaves
- 1 cup short-grain rice
- 2 tbsp. chopped parsley
- 2 tbsp. chopped mint
- 5 tbsp. olive oil
- 2 tbsp. lemon juice
- ground cinnamon
- salt and pepper
- a handful of raisins (or 1–2 cloves of garlic)

Carefully remove leaves from jar and separate under running water. Blanch the leaves briefly in boiling water, rinse, and cut off the thick stems if necessary. For the filling, wash the rice, put some oil into a pot on medium heat, add the rice, let it fry for a while, then add hot broth and let the rice simmer for 10 min. When the rice is soft, add raisins, parsley, mint, oil, salt, pepper, cinnamon, and lemon juice and mix carefully. Let the filling cool down until it can be touched. Place one leaf on a plate, veined side up, and place a scant teaspoon of the filling mixture onto the stem end of the leaf. Fold the lower sides diagonally over the filling, then roll up each package tightly. Cover the bottom of a pan with a few leaves to prevent sticking. Pour oil into the pan. Pack the stuffed leaves into the pan in tight layers. Put an inverted plate over the layers to prevent them from moving. Cover with a tight-fitting lid. Simmer gently over low heat for 10 min. and serve with slices of lemon and mint leaves.

MEAT

Meat was not a common ingredient of Near and Middle Eastern and North African cuisine until recently. Until the 1950s it was eaten only rarely and on important festive days. So one could say that the Near and Middle Eastern and North African kitchen was more or less a kitchen of vegetables. Meat was expensive, and so it was often combined with vegetables, rice, or bread, if ever used. Nevertheless, it had a long tradition, because one of the basic economic activities in the Near and Middle East and North Africa has been the herding of sheep, goats, and camels by nomadic peoples, or the raising of poultry and cows in the sedentary societies of the river systems. The animals were the source of subsistence in every way. Their milk was consumed directly or in the form of butter, cheese, or yogurt. The meat was eaten, although not too often. The hair and skin as well as intestines were used in many ways.

Beef

Cattle and buffalo were and are raised only in the river areas of the Near and Middle East and North Africa. They were used mostly as beasts of burden or draft animals. Of course, their milk was very important for the production of butter and cheese. For different reasons, the consumption of its meat was rare. First of all, cattle were normally too important for a family to slaughter them. Beef was eaten only when the animal was old and of no other use anymore. To prepare beef so that it is easy to eat demands a special knowledge. Beef requires a difficult process of ripening and refining, and this knowledge was absent in the Near and Middle East and North Africa during medieval times. Even today, not all professional cooks in the region know how to deal with beef. Because of the difficulty of preparing beef in chunks, it is often minced. In some regions, beef is cut into long strips and dried in the sun. These strips can be eaten raw or cooked. One can find this dish on the menus of some gourmet restaurants in Morocco, but the waiter will find always a way to excuse the serving of this dish. One can suspect that it does not exist at all. Some special recipes with beef, for example the Adana kebab in Turkey, consist of minced and spiced meat. The only way beef is used often is in a kind of a spicy sausage called *bastirma*. Armenians are famous all over the Near and Middle East and North Africa for how they prepare *bastirma*.

Camel

Camel was a traditional meat in the Muslim Near and Middle East and North Africa. There is a tradition that the prophet Muhammad said, "Who does not eat from my camels, is not of my people." Therefore, the consumption of camel meat has always had a religious connotation. For Jews, the meat and milk of camels were and still are taboo. The most preferred parts of this animal for eating were the humps, the stomach, and the hock. The humps store the fat, the stomach is made of different skins and muscles, and the hocks have a very muscular meat. Today, camel meat is mostly eaten by Muslims during the holy month of Ramadan, when camels for slaughtering are often imported from Somalia and South Asia to the Near and Middle East and North Africa, because the number of camels is reduced in these countries to such a degree that they are more or less a hobby of the rich. Eating camel meat today has an aspect of nostalgia, too. On the Arab peninsula, particularly, people eat it while remembering the "good old days" when they were living a free life out in the desert. In some regions, camel meat is eaten especially during wintertime, when lamb is considered too lean to be butchered. Of course, in this nostalgic context, recipes of a more complex structure are developed following older traditions—so a whole young camel is stuffed with a whole roasted lamb, which has been filled with a whole chicken. The empty cavities are filled with rice, nuts, raisins, and spices.

Fish

Although some people say that there is no tradition of fish in Near and Middle Eastern and North African cuisine, one can find many recipes with this item in ancient and modern cookbooks. Fish can be found on the shores of the Mediterranean, the Black or the Caspian Sea, the Persian Gulf, and the Indian Ocean. Fish are caught in the rivers and great lakes of the Near and Middle East and North Africa and even in the pools of the oases. The meat of most types of fish is considered ritually clean. Only those without scales, like shark, ray, or sturgeon, are seen as unclean and therefore not allowed for consumption in some parts of the Near and Middle East and North Africa, like Iran. Of course, the cooks differentiate between fish of the ocean and from fresh water. In the past, fish from deep water was considered better than that swimming beneath the surface. That fish should be fresh is known to everybody. When buying fish at the market, fishmongers will show the red gills and indicate the clear eyes of their catch.

Fish were traditionally preserved with salt. Some, however, especially small fish like anchovies, are dried in the sun and even buried in hot sand or mud for some days. When needed, the dried fish can be reconstituted by soaking in water. Today there is an elaborated system of processing fish from the catch to deep-frozen or canned form.

Looking through modern Near and Middle Eastern and North African cookbooks for recipes on fish, one can get the impression that there is no differentiation between the types of fish. Normally the main ingredient is only stated as "fish." Only rarely does one find tuna, sole, or salmon designated.

Today the preferred way to prepare fish is by grilling. The fish is eaten from head to tail, with some spices only. A very famous way of grilling has been practiced in Iraq on the sandbanks of the Euphrates and Tigris during summertime. This technique is called *masguf* (roofed). For that, a fire is lit, and the fish is placed at the side of the fire on some sticks in an upright position. The fish will be roasted very slowly and cannot be burned. In these cases, the fish, of course, must be very fresh. But fish are also used in kebabs, in stews, and as the main ingredient of soups. If fish or parts of it are fried, sunflower or sesame oil is typically used, and olive oil is avoided.

There are many ways of preparing fish besides grilling. Fish balls are made of minced fish meat combined with mashed potatoes.

Besides fish, other fruits of the sea are consumed in the Near and Middle East and North Africa. In Iran there is a discussion among the scholars of the Sharia about whether caviar is allowed. In Turkey there is no discussion about this. Fish roe puree is a part of the culinary starters. It is made using smoked roe of gray mullet. Cod's roe is a possible alternative. It is combined with strips of cucumber or cheese and garlic. Muslim scholars do not debate about other seafood. Shrimp, crab, *cigale* (sea ants), and clams are eaten, as well as lobster. Clams are often eaten raw while the other seafood is normally sautéed in butter. Cooked shrimp are also minced and formed into balls. Squid is an often-used item in the coastal kitchen.

Uskumru Dolmasi (Stuffed Mackerel)

- 1 large whole mackerel, uncleaned
- 2 onions
- 2 crushed cloves of garlic
- 3 tbsp. olive oil
- 1 tbsp. pine nuts
- 1/2 cup (60 grams) each of finely chopped almonds, hazelnuts, and walnuts
- 6 finely chopped dried apricots
- 1 tbsp. currants, soaked in water
- 1 tbsp. ground cinnamon
- 1 tbsp. ground cloves
- 1 tbsp. ground ginger, freshly chopped parsley, and chopped dill
- juice of a small lemon
- salt and pepper

Take the mackerel and cut with a sharp knife into the flesh just below the gills on the underside, as if to sever the head. Make sure that the head remains attached to the backbone. Insert your fingers down into the body and remove the guts. Clean the fish with cold running water inside and out. Take a heavy mallet and gently pound the fish up and down the body to soften the flesh and smash the backbone. Then massage and beat the skin with your hands, loosening the flesh at the same time. Be careful not to rip the skin. Squeeze from the tail end, gradually working up the fish to squeeze the mashed flesh out of the opening (similar to squeezing the last bit of toothpaste out of the tube). Reach inside to extract the bits of the backbone, and remove any small bones from the mashed flesh. Make sure that there is nothing left of the flesh to squeeze out. Once again, rinse the empty mackerel inside and out. Put aside. Pour the oil into a pan and soften the onions and the crushed garlic. Add the nuts and cook for 3 min. Add the currants, apricots, and spices, and toss the fish flesh in the mixture until it is cooked. Stir in the fresh herbs, moisten with lemon juice, and add salt and pepper. Let it cool. Now hold the empty mackerel upright in one hand and pack the stuffing through the opening, shaking the mackerel to stuff the mixture into the tail. As the cavity fills, squeeze downward to ensure the stuffing is compact. Make the mackerel resemble its natural form by squeezing and forming the fish. The stuffed mackerel is then grilled on a hot grill or baked in an oven to brown the skin. Cut the stuffed fish into slices and serve warm. Note: If only mackerel fillets are available, mash the flesh and proceed with the recipe, forming the mixture into a fish shape before baking and serving.

Game

Hunting was a favored sport in the medieval Near and Middle East and North Africa and has kept its popularity until today. In former times, arrows and lances were used. Today there are modern weapons. But in the Middle Ages, as well as today, falconry is seen as the most noble way of hunting. Muslim falconers call on God before sending the bird of prey away, so that the prey will be ritually clean and can be consumed. Objects of falconry are wild birds like wild pigeon, pheasant, and hazel-hen, and also hare and rabbit. Bigger animals such as the gazelle are, of course, hunted with rifles. Its meat is said to be very tasty. Normally the game is prepared and then grilled on an open fire in the countryside. Therefore, game meat can be bought on the market only rarely.

Fazanjoon (Wild Duck)

- 1/4 cup olive oil
- 1 medium-sized wild duck (or domestic if not available), cut into 4 parts
- 2 large onions, peeled and sliced
- 3 cups (400 gr.) ground walnuts
- 1 tbsp. whole walnuts
- 4 cups (1 l) water
- salt and pepper
- 1/2 cup (125 ml) pomegranate syrup
- 1/2 cup (125 ml) lemon juice
- 1/4 cup (50 grams) sugar
- turmeric

Heat the olive oil in a heavy pan and place the onions into it with a good pinch of dried ground turmeric. Fry for 10 min., stirring frequently until the onions are well browned. Take the onions out of the pan and place them in a large 5–6 l pot. Put the pan aside. Add the ground walnuts, water, and salt and pepper to the onions and mix carefully. Bring to a boil and then reduce the heat and let simmer for 30 min. partly covered. Put the pan back on the heat. Add more oil and heat it. Then lightly brown the four parts of the duck in the oil on all sides. Make sure that the meat is evenly browned. Now place the duck into the cooking walnut sauce. Turn the parts of the duck in the sauce, so that the meat is completely covered with the sauce. Cover the pan and let simmer for about 90 min. until the duck is nearly tender. With a spoon, remove as much of the fat as possible from the pan. Mix the pomegranate syrup, lemon juice, and sugar, and add the mixture to the sauce and duck combination. Continue cooking for another 30 min. Then place the duck onto a warmed plate and cover with the sauce. For decoration, sprinkle with pomegranate seed and whole walnuts.

Poultry

Many variants of birds were and still are part of the Near and Middle Eastern and North African cuisine. In Lebanon and other parts of the region, small birds like sparrows are grilled and eaten even with their tiny bones, which gives the impression of eating croquets. Among the wild birds, the pheasant is liked by many. Egypt is famous for its pigeons, which are raised in special houses. Also duck, geese, and turkey (originally from the Americas) and quail come into the Near and Middle Eastern and North African kitchen. Among the breeds of ancient fowl was the Chochin China fowl. The peacock, from India, was eaten in premodern times at the courts of sultans and shahs.

But the most popular breed all over the Near and Middle East and North Africa is chicken. This has been so since the Middle Ages in villages and in the folk quarters of great cities, as in the houses of the well-to-do families. In villages every family has its flock of chicken. They do not need great care and search for their food for themselves, so the cost of production is not high and can be afforded even by the poor. The proverbial popularity of chicken in the Middle Ages had its roots in the poverty and unprotected state of the peasants. Chicken were easy to acquire, easy to feed, and easy to replace when taken away by a rapacious government official or marauder. Another reason is that the meat of a chicken is cooked in a short time, so that the cost for fuel is not to high. Today chicken can be bought as a take-out food from grill stations in any big or small city of the Near and Middle East and North Africa, and on the highways they are offered to the traveler again and again. Chickens are grilled as a whole, and parts of them, like the breast, are fried or cooked. It is used in soups and stews. But these differ from what a foreigner may expect. Chicken is combined with fruit, olives, or nuts. The taste of chicken matches easily with many spices, be they hot, sour, or sweet. Chicken, like any other poultry, can be stuffed with bread, rice, herbs, and so on. The meat of chicken can even be used for a dessert.

In this case the chicken is boiled, then drained and torn into fine threads. The meat is combined with milk, cream, sugar, and rice flour. This mixture is cooked and then eaten cooled, but can, again, be put into a hot, thick-based pan, so that the bottom of the pudding is burned. Then it is cut into pieces and rolled up into logs. Because of the many options the cook has with chicken, it is called "queen of fowl."

Sheep

The meat of sheep is the most popular in Near and Middle Eastern and North African cuisine. A lamb is slaughtered on special occasions like a wedding, birth of a child, or circumcision. A rare specialty of the cuisine is the milk-fed lamb. Often families buy one or two lambs before a festival and fatten them in anticipation. Often, half of a slaughtered lamb is given to the poor. So by this a family is observing the commands of God. There is a special breed of sheep in the region, the fat-tailed sheep. The animal can store nutrients in the tail as camels do with their humps. In medieval times and today, sheep herds flock everywhere in the Near and Middle East and North Africa. Normally, the meat of a lamb of about one year of age is used, because of the quantity of fat and the quality of taste. The fat-tail is often used for frying, but also on many other cooking occasions. But all eatable parts of the lamb are used. The meat is cooked, fried, minced, and prepared in any possible way. In the Near and Middle East and North Africa, there is a saying that every possible part of the lamb should be eaten, including the head. The head is boiled in water with spices. The resulting soup is a nice warming drink on cold early mornings in the northern and mountainous regions. The meat of the sheep's head is removed and used as a topping for stock-soaked bread. The eye of a sheep is said to be a special delicacy.

FRUIT

The Near and Middle East and North Africa produce many excellent kinds of fruit. Some countries are famous for special fruits, such as Lebanon for its apples, Iraq for its dates, and Iran for pomegranates. The horticulture has been highly specialized for many centuries. Fresh fruit can be found on the market during the season, but many families in the Near and Middle East and North Africa, especially in the country, have a garden that is mainly used for growing fruit. In former times, as today, different kinds of fruit are a main export in the Near and Middle East and North Africa.

In the kitchen, fruits are used in different ways. First of all, of course, fresh fruits are consumed. Many are also cooked with sugar for jams. Others are dried and, if necessary, cut into small strips and chewed in this form for its flavor. For example, white mulberries are dried and eaten like popcorn, and dried pieces of apples are used in tea. Figs and dates are dried and conserved in this way. Fruit juices are a preferred drink.

Apples

Apples are found in many Near and Middle Eastern and North African countries. Those coming from mountain areas are preferred for their mild sour taste. Syrian apples, which were coming, in fact, from Mount Lebanon, were proverbial in earlier centuries. Today apples are still an important export of Lebanon. Apples, of course, are eaten fresh. But they are also cut into slices, dried, and seasoned with the juice of citrons. They are served with sugar, cinnamon, or even a drop of marsala. In Turkish cuisine, a cake is made with mashed cooked apples and yogurt. Apples are also combined with different kinds of meat. There are recipes with lamb and apples or beef and apples in the form of a *ragu* or soufflé. Most of these recipes are Iranian.

Apricots

Apricots are used fresh and dried. The drying is done just by spreading the fruit on the flat roof of the house. One can buy the dried fruit at the market, in special shops, and also in the supermarket. Apricots are used in many different dishes. Of course, jams are made from them, but there are combinations of apricots with bulgur and a salad with various dried fruits like raisins, apples, candied pineapples, and nuts where dried apricots play an important part. Another sweet dish is made of dried apricots cooked with the sugar and zest of lemons in water (or a white wine). Apricots are also cooked with lamb meat or in a couscous with lamb. A nice vegetarian recipe is made with cooked and minced carrots and dried apricots formed into balls and fried in hot oil.

Cherries

Cherries are found only in some Near and Middle Eastern and North African countries, like Turkey, Lebanon, Syria, and Iran. There are sweet and less sweet varieties. Cherries are like other fruit used in fresh and dried form. The sweet cherry is believed to stimulate the metabolism. In the folk medicine of the Near and Middle East and North Africa, the stalks of dried cherries are believed to have diuretic properties and, in combination with hot water, can be a remedy for hyperthermia. Even the kernels of cherries are used. In Turkey they are ground into a fine flour that is used as a flavoring in breads and cakes. Not too many recipes use cherries. Often they are used to give a contrasting sour taste in sweet dishes, and in some recipes for summer are used as a substitute for eggplant in rice dishes.

Citrons and Lemons

Citrons and lemons are, today, a very popular fruit all over the Near and Middle East and North Africa. Both the juice and the zest are used. The citrus trees had come from India to the Near and Middle East and North Africa via Oman. So, during the Middle Ages, the fruit was quite rare and very expensive. Today they are abundant and used in many different ways. They form part of dressings and improve the taste of various ingredients, vegetables, and meat in the same way. Many sweet recipes demand citrons or lemons. There are sorbets, soufflés, and fruit salads. Citrons especially are also dried. In many countries, dried citrons are kept in oil or vinegar. In Morocco there is a different way of preserving citrons. There is a special variety of citrons with thin skins grown in the Sous plains in southern Morocco. For three days the fruit is covered with cold water. Then the citrons are cut into four parts lengthwise, but in such a way that they are sticking together on the lower part. The quarters are torn apart a little and filled with salt. Then they are put into a glass pot, more salt is added on top of the fruit, and the juice of a citron is dripped on top of that. Then the pot is filled with cooking water. The fruits should be covered completely. The citrons can be used after three weeks and will be usable for three months. These salted citrons are combined with meat (chicken, for example) and give a very special flavor.

Dates

The most famous fruit of all the Near and Middle East and North Africa is, of course, the date. This fruit can be found everywhere, and if it cannot grow for climatic reasons, it is imported. Date palms swaying in the wind are synonymous with the Western image of the Near and Middle East and North Africa. Dates are among the oldest horticultural plants of the world. For generations, the people of the Near and Middle East and

Dates.

North Africa, especially the nomads, were living mostly on this fruit. As the proverb goes, "The date needs her head in the heat of the sun and her foot in the water." Therefore, they are found in the great river valleys and in the oases of the deserts.

Dates are eaten by rich and poor, in fresh and dried forms. Fresh dates can be frozen. Dried dates are particularly nutritious. Dates are rich in protein, sugar, and iron, potassium, and magnesium. For Muslims, dates have a special meaning, because there is a tradition that the prophet Muhammad liked them and broke the Ramadan fasting with a date. Medieval cookbooks report some simple ways of preparing fresh dates. The pit was removed and replaced with a nut such as an almond. Modern cooks have filled dates with cheese or even ham (of course, not in Muslim countries). Dates are also filled with mixtures of sugar, fine-chopped onions, and rose water. One simple recipe goes like this: The flesh is taken out of a big melon. Its juice is kept. Then dried dates are put into the empty melon and the melon juice is added. After a time the dates have the taste of melon.

Dates are today the basic ingredient of many sweets and jams. Of course, dates, especially dried ones, are also added to lamb meat or chicken, giving a honeylike taste.

Figs

The other famous fruit of the Near and Middle East and North Africa is the fig, although for climatic reasons it does not grow everywhere, so dried figs are imported. They are nutritious and rich in glucose, potassium, and vitamins. Because of their form, there is the rumor that figs can be used as an aphrodisiac. The fact that the white flesh of the fruit turns red when ripe is compared to the male sperm, which is white, and the red flesh of a human being developing from that. There are also many magical rites, especially in love affairs, but figs also play a part in traditional medicine. A woman in labor eats a fig first thing in the morning to convince the baby to come to the world.

There are mainly two types of figs: those that have green skin and those that have blue skin. The color has nothing to do with the degree of ripeness. There are many variants and types of dried figs. Well known are the mini-figs with a very intensive taste that come from Iran and Turkey. Figs are often consumed fresh, perhaps in a combination with other fruit in a fruit salad, but figs can be also be a part of a salad made of dry fruit. They are kept in flavored water for about 48 hours beforehand.

Grapes

Grapes have always been important in the regions. Although wine is normally forbidden for Muslims, grapes are still produced. Either they are dried and raisins are exported, for example, from Yemen, or they are exported fresh from Turkey, Lebanon, and North Africa to Europe by air. In some countries, in spite of the religious regulations, wine is produced from grapes for the tourist industries and for export. In fact, Algeria is the largest producer of red wines in the world. Most of this wine goes to France.

Melons

Melons of various kinds, especially watermelons, are a part of the normal summer diet of many people in the Near and Middle East and North Africa. With their high percentage of water content, they are very thirst quenching. They are among the very old fruits of the Near and Middle East and North Africa. From Assyrian times, there are pictures of melons on reliefs. The Old Testament says that melons were one of the things that allowed the people of Israel to survive the desert. Melons are mostly eaten raw, sometimes as part of a fruit salad. In olden times they were cut into pieces and dried. It seems that melons were not cooked.

Oranges

Oranges, like citrons, are relatively new to the Near and Middle East and North Africa. They were also imported from India in the eighth century. Today they are one of the most important agricultural exports from the Near and Middle East and North Africa to Europe. Orange juice is very popular. Oranges are used fresh in fruit salads and in sweet dishes and jams and are added to lamb or a tabbouleh with lentils. Near and Middle Easterners and North Africans are very fond of orange-flower water. That is a product of the distillation of the flowers and leaves of special orange trees. It is used for refreshment after a meal by sprinkling it on the hands and face. Traditional medicine maintains that this expensive water is a sedative and provides a healthy sleep. Some drops of this liquid into a cake, a soufflé, or ice cream will give a very special flavor.

Pomegranates

Pomegranates are also an often-used fruit in the cuisine of the Near and Middle East and North Africa. The trove of ruby-red grains, concealed within a tough, leathery skin, still symbolizes fertility, good fortune, and the continuity of life. Pomegranates are also considered a cleansing fruit, able to lift the soul and diminish negative feeling. The juice of pomegranates is used for seasoning many dishes instead of lemon juice and can be used as a drink. A syrup (*dibs rumman*) is made of pomegranate seeds and is added to many dishes, especially those with duck or another fat meat.

NUTS

Near and Middle Easterners and North Africans adore nuts. Nuts are used in many ways. They are eaten fresh (some even green), ripe, and fried. One can find them in sweet and salty dishes, in salads, and pounded into sauces. Predominantly they are part of fillings of vegetables, chicken, or fish. Because they are very nourishing, they are used as a remedy for thin or weak children, who, in Turkey, are treated every morning with a spoonful of chopped pine nuts, walnuts, and raisins mixed with ground cinnamon.

Almonds

The most popular type of nut is the almond. Almonds have been known since pre-Islamic times in the Near and Middle East and North Africa. Almonds are seen as a symbol of beauty, depicted in ceramics, miniatures, and paintings. In the kitchen they are used in different ways. There is a soup with almonds, pounded almonds, and chicken broth. They are added to vegetarian dishes at the end of the cooking process, just before serving.

They are also used in meat and fish dishes. One recipe combines almonds and yogurt with pieces of chicken. Of course, pounded almonds are used in sweet dishes like puddings and baked into biscuits and cakes, often in combination with dates. There is, of course, also the famous almond milk. It is prepared from pounded almonds, sugar, the rind of an orange, and water. This drink is served very cold. It is said that bathing in almond milk increases the beauty of a person.

Chestnuts

Chestnuts are found mainly in the mountains and less hot regions of the Near and Middle East and North Africa. They are freshly roasted, sold in the streets as a special winter snack, and used in the kitchen with some vegetables. They can substitute for potatoes.

Hazelnuts

More common than chestnuts are hazelnuts, which are also found in mountain areas like the region of the Black Sea in Turkey. Harvested, they are dried along the roads and then sold in the markets. They are also an important export for countries such as Turkey. In the kitchen they are used in many ways. Normally they are pounded and added to a special sauce with olive oil and garlic to accompany vegetables, fish, and meat. Hazelnuts are also an important ingredient of sweets, such as cookies and the famous halvah.

Pine Nuts

Pine nuts are the most expensive of all nuts in the Near and Middle East and North Africa, because it is not easy to remove the firm, thin shell. These nuts are often used roasted, when they develop a special taste. They are needed for salads, fillings, or roasted meat. They are also pounded and added to fillings.

Pistachios

Pistachios are a nice snack, and are often served with a cup of coffee or tea. In that case they are roasted in their shell, which opens up during roasting, and then salted. They are also used in sweet and salty dishes.

Pistachios.

Sunflower Seeds

Sunflower seeds are not nuts, but they are used as snacks like some of the nuts mentioned. In simple tea houses, they are served with tea or coffee, and the customers open the seed with their teeth and spit the shells on the ground. Some people are convinced that sunflower seeds have a protective quality against prostrate problems.

Walnuts

Walnuts in some languages of the region are called "the king of nuts." Of course, they can be found in a less subtropical climate. They grow mainly in Turkey and Iran. There they are eaten even green, especially by young boys who climb up the trees and eat them right there. Walnuts are an important export for these two countries. They are used in the kitchen in combination with sweet and salty ingredients. Pounded, they are made into sauces with olive oil and garlic to accompany vegetables, fish, and meat.

DAIRY

In cultures and societies where the nomadic way of life played an important role, like that of the Near and Middle East and North Africa, there must be a culinary tradition that has to do with milk and its products. So it does not come as a surprise that the milk of cows, sheep, goats, and camels are important drinks. Milk, mostly cow milk, is consumed fresh. This milk is consumed cold, but also hot or with ingredients that are said to have special benefits. A little spring of marjoram in heated milk will give one a good night's rest. But there is a special cult in Arab countries of the peninsula where camel milk is very much appreciated. Though nourishing, the camel milk is also said to be purgative and can be used in this way only. It is impossible to produce butter or other milk products from this milk.

Milk has a strong symbolic aspect in Near and Middle Eastern and North African cultures. Its white color symbolizes purity. Because of its nourishing qualities, milk is drunk by young women with the yolk of an egg and fenugreek. Because of its color, it is seen as a messenger of happiness. Like sugar or eggs, because of its white glimmering color it is compared to silver coins. That is why milk is used as a magic device for procuring welfare and happiness. So, among the Jews of North Africa, the mother of the bride-groom hands a glass of milk and a piece of sugar to the bride. She has to eat the sugar and drink some of the milk; then she throws the rest of the milk on the ground. Later the bride has to break a jar with milk, thereby ensuring the love of her husband. In combination with cinnamon, butter, asparagus, and egg yolk, milk is said to have aphrodisiac qualities.

Milk from cows, sheep, or goats was and is also used in a fermented form. This sour type of milk is drunk and is very thirst quenching. In some countries, like Morocco, it is a typical drink in the month of fasting. Sour milk is also added to various dishes. It gives a sour taste to meat and vegetables. The most famous type of fermented milk, of course, is yogurt. Although Arabs claim today that it was invented by them, the word comes from the Turkish language. Yogurt is rich in minerals and vitamins, provides an easily digestible source of calcium, and contains antibiotic properties. There are different types of yogurt in different countries and regions, which depends, of course, on the quality of the milk. Some cooks insist that the yogurt of goat milk is the best one can find. Blended with water, yogurt makes a refreshing drink, which is called *ayran* in Turkey, but can also be found in other countries. Yogurt can be seasoned with garlic and herbs and then can be a part of a *mezze* and combined with honey, fresh fruit, and/or cinnamon in a light desert. Added to meat and vegetable dishes, it gives a special gusto, typical for Turkish, Lebanese, or Syrian cuisine.

Many types of white cheese made from sheep milk are also very popular in Near and Middle Eastern and North African cuisine. It can be soft or hard and is more or less salty. If the cheese contains too much salt, it is soaked for a time before eating. That is why one can see this cheese in water basins on the market. It is eaten with black olives or jam and honey for the breakfast; added to many types of stews; and is part of the many fillings, like pancakes with spinach.

FATS

There are various types of fat in Near and Middle Eastern and North African cuisine. Which one is used depends on the religious affiliation of the cook and the eater and, of course, also on the taste.

Animal Fat

There is one more often-used fat, which is an animal fat. It is made from the rendered fat of a special sheep. This sheep, which can be found in all the herds wandering through the countryside between Morocco and Afghanistan, has a tail that grows to an enormous size. It consists almost entirely of fat. It is cooked slowly in liquid form in small pots, where it can harden. Later it can be used for frying. Added to vegetables, it has a saturating effect. For many, the flavor of this fat has been improved by adding meat, pieces of apples, quinces, onions, cinnamon, mastic, dill, and many other flavors. It has always been quite expensive, and is therefore used in small doses only. Looking through modern cookbooks of Near and Middle Eastern and North African cuisine, one may get the impression that the fat of the sheep tail is nearly out of use. On the other hand, the number of herds of fat-tail sheep in the Near and Middle East and North Africa has not diminished. Therefore one should suspect that it is still in quite a general use.

Argania Oil

There is one special oil used mostly in Morocco that should be mentioned. It is the oil of the fruit of the argania tree. Traveling through the southern parts of Morocco, one will see a strange picture: there are goats climbing into trees. These argania trees are to be found only in the triangle between the cities of Essaouira, Agadir, and Taroudant, south of the High Atlas. For the inhabitants of this region, this tree is a miracle. It grows in a semidesert region and gives a consumable oil. But this oil is produced in a complicated way. Goats and sometimes camels eat the fruit of this tree, which has the size and color of apricots, and later spit the kernels out. Shepherds, women, and children collect them. The kernels are crushed with a hand-mill of stone, and the oil is collected. It has a very special, nutty taste. It is more fatty than olive oil and has a color that tends toward brown. Argania oil is said to be an aphrodisiac. It is consumed lukewarm with bread as a snack. Normally it is used for seasoning salads and cold dishes. It is also used for special Moroccan sweets.

Butter

Butter of the milk of cows, sheep, and goats was used as a fat only rarely. Butter can be preserved longer than milk. It is produced by agitating the milk until it becomes hard. This was done in the skins of goats. But more durable in conservation is a special product of the butter of cow milk, that is, clarified butter (ghee, or *samn*) that is used in the Near and Middle Eastern and North African kitchen often. It can be kept for many months without an icebox. The price of this fat was so high that it was sold by the spoonful. It is very simple to produce it. The butter is clarified by simmering it for half an hour. By this the water in the butter will evaporate, and the salt and sediments can be scooped off. Ghee is used for frying meat, potatoes, and other ingredients and gives a special flavor distinct from butter.

Olive Oil

Perhaps the most often-used fat is olive oil. Olive trees are found in many countries of the Near and Middle East and North Africa. Since pre-Islamic times, olives have been grown and olive oil produced in the regions of Syria, Lebanon, some parts of Iraq, Iran, Turkey, and North Africa. For Muslims the olive tree is a symbol of the light and of the prophethood. How important olive trees are for the cuisine of the Near and Middle East and North Africa can be shown by a proverb. A mother gives advice to her daughter and says, "Marry him, although he is old. He is the owner of olive trees."

Olives were and still are an important export product. Green olives are the unripe fruit, and only the black ones are ripe. Both green and black olives are conserved in a brine or marinated in olive oil with additional herbs and spices to be served as starters. Picking olives is a very tiring task. The trees are beaten with long sticks so that the olives fall down. Then the farmers search for every single fruit and collect them into baskets, typically made of willow branches. Children are often engaged for this, too. After that, the fruits are sprinkled with coarse salt and kept in containers for up to a week. During this time they must be turned regularly in the salt. By this procedure, the skin and the flesh become softer.

Olives can also be filled with an almond instead of the olive pit. As an appetizer, they can be combined with chickpeas or oranges, as a salad with carrots. Black olives are also added to some meat stews, which gives them a special taste. The olive pits are strung together and make a rosary for devout Muslims. In traditional medicine, olives are said to give virile power and be helpful for problems of the gall bladder and digestion.

Most important is, of course, the oil made of the olives in a process that has been known since time immemorial. Today this oil is produced in a traditional way in many places in the Near and Middle East and North Africa. Normally one needs five kilograms of fruit for one liter of oil. The fruits with their flesh and pits are crushed with great millstones into a dark pulp. This is pressed into sieves made of intertwined grass or plastic. The liquid is collected in tubes of different material. After some time, the water and oil separate. The oil is on the top of the tube, so that it can be scooped of easily. Today many companies produce olive oil with modern techniques. The pulp is pressed several times to extract all liquids. The oil that is extracted with the fourth pressing is used for cosmetic products like soaps and shampoos. The dry remains of the pressing are used as a fertilizer, and the wood of the tree makes wonderful bowls. In many regional cuisines, olive oil is used as the most-preferred oil for many recipes with rice, couscous, or omelets. Often it is consumed with just some bread as a breakfast. But the use of this oil is relatively recent. Only in the seventeenth century was it used in the palace kitchen of the Sultan at Istanbul. Until then it was only used for the lamps of the mosques. But then it found its way into kitchens all over the Near and Middle East and North Africa.

Olives.

Today, there is a discussion about the overall use of olive oil, because it has its own flavor, which may change the taste of other ingredients of a dish. But traditionally it is most often used, especially in vegetable recipes and in the famous *mezze*, in the kitchens of Muslims. As is well known, it is a very healthy type of oil, as long as it is not heated over 100°C, when it changes its structure and is comparable to the fat of animals. For dishes where high-temperature fat is needed or where the flavor should not be masked by the oil, normally today sunflower oil is used.

Sesame-Seed Oil

Sesame-seed oil is produced from the seed of the sesame plant. About half of this seed consists of oil. This oil is nearly tasteless and is therefore used for dishes with ingredients that have a delicate flavor. In former times it was hard to preserve this oil. Therefore it was rarely used. This has changed, and today the oil and especially the remains of the process of production, the famous *tahîna*, are often-used ingredients.

SEASONINGS AND SPICES

Near and Middle Eastern and North African cuisine is so rich in spices and seasonings that one may despair of describing them all. They are often combined in mixtures of seasonings by the individual taste of a housewife or a producer. A medieval cookbook has categorized the different tastes and flavor used in that cuisine in 10 different groups. One can follow this structure even today, as nearly all of the spices and herbs mentioned by this book are still used.

Fragrant Spices

Cardamom

Cardamom is an often-used spice in the kitchens of the Near and Middle East and North Africa. It has a tradition that reaches back to the times of the Assyrian kings before Islam. Traditionally it is said that it helps digestion and protects against flatulence. And since the time of the tales of *The Thousand and One Nights*, its aphrodisiac power has been known. Cardamom has a very intense odor. The capsules are used whole, crushed, grounded; in Morocco its fresh green is also added to some dishes. Cardamom is used for fish, meat, and sweets. Some capsules are put into the coffee, which gives a very special taste.

Kapalisarsi Grand Bazaar spice market, Istanbul, Turkey. © Art Directors/TRIP Helene Rogers.

Cinnamon

In the first group are ingredients that give an odor or perfume to the dish. Of the most popular spices that give an odor or perfume to the dish in Near and Middle Eastern and North African cuisine is cinnamon, which is the dried bark of the cassia tree. Its flowery flavor makes it understandable that it is categorized as a fragrant spice. Tradition says that it "warms" the dishes.

There are two ways of using it. In most cases, the ground form is common, but cinnamon sticks are also added to a dish and taken away after the cooking. As cinnamon can become old quickly and in that state spoils a dish, cookbooks admonish the cook to only use it fresh. It is used in the modern kitchen of the Near and Middle East and North Africa not only in sweet dishes, but also in rice and in combination with meat. For example, in Morocco, the famous *bstilla* with doves is spiced with cinnamon. Cinnamon is also added to tomato sauces and even fish. Cinnamon is also added to coffee, because of the taste. But there is also a medical reason. Traditional medicine says that cinnamon improves the circulation of blood and the digestion. It is good against fatigue and, of course, is an aphrodisiac. Cinnamon has a beneficial effect in the liver and counterbalances the negative influence of coffee on this organ. A drink is made with cinnamon sticks and water, which are heated together. The hot liquid is sweetened with sugar.

Cloves

Cloves are a very common spice in Near and Middle Eastern and North African cuisine. During the Middle Ages, it was not known where they came from. Rumors said that they were bought in "silent trade." In traditional medicine it was already known that cloves had positive results, especially against tooth pain. Whole cloves are chewed to freshen the breath. Today it is known that cloves have disinfecting capacities. Cloves also have a strong scent. They are to be found in different recipes, in crushed form and whole. They are mainly used in meat casseroles, sweets, breads, and pastries.

Fenugreek

The seeds of fenugreek are also counted under the heading of fragrant spices. Traditionally, it is known to help gain weight. Generally, it was believed that fenugreek brings back the joy of living. In the kitchen it is often used fresh and cut into pieces. The stamen is sprinkled onto loaves of bread before baking.

Galangal

Galangal, a spice near to ginger with a peppery taste, is used in the Near and Middle Eastern and North African kitchen. It is imported from China. Housewives are admonished to see that the roots have no black spots and are mold-free. It is often added to fish or chicken.

Mastic

Mastic, the resin of the mastic tree (*Pistacia lenticus*), is in the category of fragrant spices because it has a somewhat negative effect. It is used to quench or cover the overwhelming taste of another ingredient. Normally it is used in powder form and added to bread and cakes. Mastic resin is also chewed like chewing gum and gives fresh breath.

Nard

Nard is imported from India. Its scent is compared with that of apples. It is used in producing perfumes. At least in the Middle Ages, nard must have been expensive, because traders had tricks to adulterate it.

Nutmeg

An intense scent is also to be found with nutmeg, but this spice is not very much in use; it mostly appears in combination with sweet dishes.

Rose Petals

For centuries in the Near and Middle East and North Africa, the scented petals of pink and red roses have been infused in oil, milk, sugar, and water and used especially in sweet dishes. They are cooked in a syrup so that they are covered with this sugar, which keeps them for a time. These petals are put on top of special sweets like the famous *katayef*, which is pancakes layered with cream. When the sugar crystallizes, the rose petals change their flavor in a negative way. Often used is rose water, which is a liquid distilled from rose petals. It was and still is very expensive.

Saffron

Saffron is also rubricated under the heading of fragrant spices. Its delicate light flavor gives a special character to many dishes. The dried stamen of the yellow crocus is the most expensive spice in the world. The best saffron comes from Yemen. Great quantities are imported from Catalunia, Andalusia, and Tuscany. Today, saffron is produced in greater quantities, but it is still hard work and is done mostly by hand. That is why it is still expensive. But it is not only the flavor that is important for Near and Middle Eastern and North African cuisine. Small quantities give a nice red-yellow color to many dishes. It is used for bread and cakes, as well as soups, fish, and various types of meat and rice. Because of its price, there is a long tradition of counterfeiting this expensive spice. It was and is diluted with cheaper products like curcuma, which has the advantage that it gives a yellow color to dishes like saffron. Saffron can be combined with red pepper, salt, and even sand to falsify it.

Dried Fruits and Pits

Another category of flavorings or spices consists of dried fruit and pits. Concerning pits, almonds are the most preferred, although they are not cheap. In Near and Middle Eastern and North African cuisine, they are used in peeled form only. They are added to stews of vegetables, meat, and chicken, and also with fried fish as whole pits. For sauces they are cut into smaller pieces or even ground. Walnuts and hazelnuts are less expensive. Normally they are added to the dishes in chopped or ground form. Looking through many recipes, one gets the impression that walnuts are used more often than hazelnuts. Normally these nuts and almonds are not combined. Of course, pine nuts and pistachios are used as a kind of seasoning. Besides pits, dried fruit is understood as another kind of seasoning. Often used are dried jujubes, which are more sweet dry than fresh. Raisins and dried dates and figs are also understood as spices.

Fresh Fruit

Fresh fruit is also considered a special category of flavorings. It is important to mention that there is a difference between sweet and sour fruit of the same kind. That means that there is a distinction between sweet and sour pomegranates, or between sweet and sour apples. Unripe berries are also used. There are also sweet fruit like melons, bananas, and apricots used to give a special taste. But generally, one can say that it is more the sour variants that are used to give this flavor to the dishes.

Sweeteners

The Near and Middle East and North Africa is famous for its sweet dishes. So ingredients that sweeten dishes are an important group of flavorings. First of all, sugar is the main sweetener. Sugar cane has a long tradition in the region and is used in different ways. In most cases one can buy ground white sugar and also sugar loaves. Sugar has no special taste except its sweetness. It is cooked with water into a syrup and used to soak cakes and similar dishes. There is also brown sugar, which has a special taste besides its sweetness. There is also palm sugar, which is produced by cutting the tree and collecting the liquid that comes out of the cut. This liquid is heated so that the water evaporates. One gets a sweet and sticky mass that is used in some recipes in the eastern part of the Arab world and in Iran.

Traditionally, honey is a more preferred sweetener. It is more expensive, because it cannot be produced everywhere in the Near and Middle East and North Africa. Countries like Turkey or Iran and some parts of Lebanon and Syria, as well as the mountains of the Atlas in Morocco, have a rich production. These honeys have different colors, from a creamy white over yellow and gold to dark brown. Honey is used to sweeten various dishes, especially cakes and desserts. Often it is eaten in sticky dollops on fresh bread or dripped over yogurt. But it is also added to some salty dishes like fish. Honey is seen as a symbol for happiness and is said to ward off sadness. A young wife will put some honey on her hands before she prepares couscous for the first time for her family, so that the tenderness of the honey will influence her. It is used as a remedy to cure many diseases that occur the winter. Honey plays an important part in some magic rituals. In Moroccan villages, if a woman wants to attract a certain man, she puts some honey on her forehead and lets it flow down over her nose and lips, collects it with a spoon, and adds a drop of her blood and seven corns of salt. This mixture is given to the man, who should drink it.

Sour Spices

The spices in this category give a sour taste to the dishes. There is, of course, vinegar made of grapes or other fruit. Many a Near and Middle Eastern and North African housewife also prepares herbal vinegars. A very special ingredient to sour a dish is sumac. It is a powder from the fruit of the sumac tree (*Rhus coriaria*), and it is more often used than vinegar. It comes in berry form or ground. The berries grow wild in many parts of the Near and Middle East and North Africa. They are harvested, then soaked in water for a time. After that they are pressed to squeeze out the juice, which can be used as a marinade for fish or chicken. Ground sumac is sprinkled on salads or added to fish, meat, soups, and rice dishes. If sumac is not available, the juice of lemon or citron is used instead. In addition to giving an acid taste to the dish, it cuts the heaviness of olive oil. The fresh or dried leaves of lemons or citrons give a delicate, mild sour taste to many dishes.

Vegetables and Herbs

Vegetables and herbs are another important category of flavorings and spices. The foremost of them is the onion. Onions come in many different forms and colors of different tastes and are produced nearly year-round. Almost all Near and Middle Eastern and North African recipes contain onions. There is even a combination with honey, a sweet kind of onion syrup, almost a marmalade, that is added to fish or meat. Onions are also pressed so that the liquid can be used to marinate fish or meat. Even the stamen of onions is used for some dishes. Onions still play an important role in medicine. Traditionally, they were said to lengthen life, and they are believed to be an aphrodisiac. Modern medicine has found that they have positive characteristics indeed. Onions lower high blood pressure and are rich in vitamins A, B, and C, and calcium and potassium.

From the same botanical family as onions comes garlic. The use of garlic in the cuisine of the Near and Middle East and North Africa is a topic of many discussions among cooks and housewives. In these arguments, magical and medical aspects play a role. It is believed that garlic wards off the evil eye. And not only in folk medicine is it thought to improve the circulation of the blood and thus help to lower high blood pressure. Surprisingly, garlic is not generally used in great quantities in recipes from the region. Garlic is used in different forms: fresh or dried, pickled whole in its skin, or fried in its skin together with meat or fish. In some recipes, great quantities are used. There are garlic soups, or salads with yogurt, where it plays an important role. Smaller quantities are needed in combination with vegetables that have only a slight taste, such as zucchini or eggplant. And there are recipes where garlic is a vegetable—for example, chicken with great quantities of unskinned garlic. The extensive use of garlic seems to be a phenomenon of a more peasant cuisine with simple and strong tastes. The bourgeois kitchen of the Near and Middle East and North Africa, however, uses only small quantities of garlic, if any. Cookbooks give advice on how to avoid garlic breath.

The use of other herbs has strong regional aspects. In some countries, herbs are one of the most important flavors and are used in nearly any dish; in others they are only one among others. This has to do, of course, with the fact that herbs are best when they are fresh. In regions where herbs are not easy to grow because of the climate, they do not play an important part in the kitchen. Where they grow abundantly, they are used in great quantities. One of these herbs is coriander. Traditional medicine reported that coriander wards off melancholia and helps with digestion. Coriander seeds are used in crushed form in the Turkish kitchen in some of the highly flavored dishes. In Moroccan cuisine, fresh coriander leaves are used in so many recipes that one can say that it is the typical flavor of Moroccan food. There it is also used mixed with garlic, pepper, parsley, lemon juice, and oil in the famous *chermoula* sauce. It is added to many warm and cold dishes, and especially to fish. In countries like Egypt or Iraq and on the Arab peninsula, its use is comparatively rare.

Parsley is another often-needed herb. It is always flat-leaved and tasty. Traditionally, it is thought that it is good for countering menstruation cramps; that it is calming; and that if it is given regularly to a child, he or she will become strong and healthy. In the Turkish kitchen it is used in great quantities, not only to flavor dishes, but even as a salad—for example, in the famous tabbouleh, a salad with parsley and bulgur.

Another herb is mint, again typical for Morocco and Turkey. Mint is used fresh or dried in salads, vegetable dishes, and stews. In Turkey it is combined with yogurt and makes a refreshing dip; in North Africa fresh leaves are put into tea. There is also the interesting combination of mint with spinach. Basil is an herb of the Turkish kitchen and the Fertile Crescent. It is used in fresh and dry form for salads and especially seafood dishes. Dill is an often-used herb in Turkish cuisine. It is eaten fresh on its own to freshen the breath, and accompanies fish. In other regional cuisines it is very rare. Thyme, like oregano, is used in many regional cuisines, but only rarely is it used on its own. Mostly it is an important ingredient of spice mixtures.

Tabbouleh

- 1–3 oz. (25–75 grams) fine *burgul* (bulgur wheat, 4 oz. [100 grams])
- finely chopped parsley
- 5 tbsp. finely chopped mint
- 5 tbsp. finely chopped spring onions
- 3 tomatoes, seeded and finely chopped
- 4 tbsp. olive oil
- 3 tbsp. fresh lemon juice
- 1 tbsp. salt

Soak *burgul* in water for about 20 minutes until al dente. Drain and squeeze out the excess moisture. Add the *burgul* to onions, parsley, and mint. Mix olive oil, lemon juice, and salt and add it onto the salad. Let it stand for 15 min. so that the flavors may be absorbed. Add the tomatoes. Toss the salad. (More adventurous eaters may add some raisins soaked in water or juice for half an hour.)

General Spices

One more group of spices and seasonings are generally required ingredients that give flavor. The main one, of course, is salt. It is used in a raw form and is very fine. The quality is seen by its whiteness. The more white, the better. The Near and Middle East and North Africa have nearly no sources of stone salt. So the greatest quantities are produced on the shores of the Mediterranean, the Gold Sea, the Red Sea, and the Atlantic. Even today, while traveling along the Lebanese seashore, one finds the basins where the seawater is dried to get the small quantities of salt. But generally, stone salt is now imported to the Near and Middle East and North Africa.

Personal Mixtures

Then there are mixtures of different spices and herbs that are prepared by the housewives or bought by them at the market. Every cook has his or her own recipe and often keeps it as a secret. He or she does not even give it to daughters or relatives. That is why it took time until Western observers of Near and Middle Eastern and North African culinary culture understood what the names of certain spices were. One typical example for this situation is *za'tar*. It is a mixture of many herbs and spices, among them thyme. The various cookbooks differ in their recipes for *za'tar*. It is used very often in the kitchens of the Fertile Crescent, in Iraq, and on the Arab peninsula. In North Africa it is unknown. One finds *za'tar* to be a mixture of sesame seeds, dried thyme, and dried oregano in equal parts, the seeds browned in a pan without fat; all ingredients are crushed and ground to become more or less pulverized. Another recipe adds sumac; cooked, dried, unsalted chickpeas, also pulverized; marjoram instead of oregano; salt; and so on. This mixture is given as a kind of allspice to many dishes or sprinkled on the dough of bread and baked, but it can also be mixed with olive oil and dripped on yogurt.

Another mixture is called *ras al-hanut*, which means "head of the shop" or "the best of the shop." As the name indicates, normally it is bought in the market in shops specializing in spices, flavors, perfumes, and traditional medical items. It is the most famous spice mixture in North Africa. There are very many combinations and variations depending on the likes and dislikes of the seller, the time of the year when it is combined, the quality of the available ingredients, and the demand of the buyers; it is normally hot, but the degree is different. That is why *ras al-hanut* is considered to be a spice of wintertime, although it is used year-round. It should be composed of at least 12 ingredients. Because of the many ingredients, which differ in price, the price of *ras al-hanut* can be twice as much as that of a simple mixture. It can contain pepper, *melegueta* pepper (grains of paradise), lavender, thyme, rosemary, cumin, ginger, nutmeg, mace, cardamom, clove, fenugreek, and cinnamon. There are even strange ingredients like rosebuds, root of violet, a special kind of rue (*pega-num harmala*), belladonna, and Spanish fly (cantharides). *Ras al-hanut* is used in many dishes as an allspice, but especially with sweeter variants of chicken recipes, stews, and the sauce that is added to the North African main dish, couscous.

Another Near and Middle Eastern and North African spice mixture is called *bahharat,* which originally means "spices" and contains grounded rosebuds and cinnamon in North Africa. In the Fertile Crescent, the same name is given to the dried berries of the pimento tree. The taste is said to be a combination of cinnamon, cloves, and nutmeg. It is used with meat dishes and sweets.

There is also a hot sauce that could be seen as a trademark of the North African cuisine. It is called *harisa*. As the main ingredient of this spice is chili, it is clear that it is a newcomer to the kitchen of Morocco and Tu-nisia. In Algeria it is not common. *Harisa* is found all over the Near and Middle East and North Africa as a kind of hot allspice. The use varies in the named North African countries. In Tunisia, for example, it is stirred into nearly every dish except sweets; in Morocco it is served separately, so that every eater can chose how much of it he or she will use. Many housewives prepare *harisa* for their family at home, but it can be bought ready-made and is also available in canned form. The degree of hotness depends on the chilies. If it should not be too hot, one chooses chilies with a mild hotness, and for a hot *harisa*, of course, a hot type of chili. The chilies are dried and cut into small pieces and soaked in warm water for half an hour. The chili is pressed from the water and mixed with olive oil, garlic, salt, and cumin. All this is put into a cutter and worked into a soft paste. Normally it is put into a clean glass and some olive oil is added on top. The *harisa* can be kept up to six months. This sauce is added to all piquant dishes, but especially to soups and fish.

Iran also has its special spicing mixture. It is called *kashk* and is a kind of dried yogurt. Its production is complicated and can be done only in summertime in the dry climate of central Iran. The yogurt is salted and its cream is taken off. Then the yogurt is put into a sack of cotton and hung on the branch of a tree or something like that for three to four days to loosen its liquid. From the rest of the yogurt small clods are made, which are dried more on cotton towels in the sun until they are completely dry and hard. Now they can be stored for years. If one wanted to use these clods of *kashk,* which looked like limestone in former times, one had to soak them overnight. The next day the result was put into a sieve, dried and then ground. The resulting powder was put in water or added to a dish by the spoonful. Today *kashk* is sold in the market in pulverized form and dissolves easily in water and then is added to various soups.

Coloring Agents

Traditional cooking in the Near and Middle East and North Africa considered coloring agents to be spices. In haute cuisine there has been, and now is again, a tendency to give certain colors to dishes. The old cuisine used colorings such as the powder of lapis lazuli for blue. Today in Near and Middle Eastern and North African haute cuisine, colorful dishes are also popular. But now, besides the original color of ingredients like the red of tomato or red pepper and green of spinach, food colors are used.

DRINKS

Water is, of course, the most important drink in the Near and Middle East and North Africa. People drink it in great quantities. They know that it is indispensable for life. As in many other desert or semiarid regions, giving water to a thirsty person is an absolute must for anybody, almost like a religious duty. Normally water is consumed cool. For this cooling there are many modern and traditional techniques. Traditionally water is stored in big jars of clay, often covered with a piece of textile or the leaves of a tree, the branch of a palm, or a stone. The water evaporates through the clay very slowly. This evaporation brings a cooling effect for the water. By this technique, the water is not too much cooled down, so that it is very pleasant and refreshing to drink. But, of course, today, normally the modern cooling methods are used, such as refrigerators. In restaurants water is served with ice to keep it cool. But water is a rare item in the region. Therefore, in history as today it is the reason for political strife and even wars.

In many regions water is polluted, so that it must be cooked, filtered, or chemically cleaned. Because of the different qualities of water, the people of the Near and Middle East and North Africa have developed criteria for drinking water. They prefer, of course, drinking water that is provided by central agencies with pipes. This tap water should be drinkable without any treatment. If this cannot be provided by the state or the municipality, it is seen as a major obstacle to the political acceptance of a political regime. But even if there is tap water, many people use water from springs for drinking. They bring this water themselves in balloons and tanks to their homes. In countries like Oman or Turkey, on weekends many families fetch water from certain springs, driving more than an hour by car. People discuss which water of which spring is more acceptable. Spring water is thought to be more healthful than tap water, although this may not be true. Drinking water is also provided by companies who sell it in bottles. Here one finds private firms and state-owned ones side by side. The water is said to be conveyed from sources deep under the surface. It has, usually, the name of a famous spring of the country.

Alcohol

Although alcoholic drinks are forbidden for Muslims, there is no prohibition in most Near and Middle Eastern and North African countries. Only in very few countries, like Saudi Arabia and the former North Yemen, are alcoholic drinks completely forbidden, so those people who are addicted to alcohol have to take illegal measures to get their drinks. There is a lot of smuggling and moonlight production of strong alcoholic drinks in these countries, and the prices are extremely high. Many other countries of the region have their own breweries. In many cases they were established by German, Austrian, Dutch, and other European companies. The beer they produce has a lesser amount of alcohol than the types with the same name in Europe. But there are also beers with names in Near and Middle Eastern and North African languages, like an Iraqi beer called Ferida. But there is also imported beer on the market. Normally this beer is sold in bottles. There is no draft beer. Beer is not consumed openly, but rather either at home or in clubs. In some countries there were and still are locations in side streets where beer is sold, and, of course, it is sold in night clubs and places like that.

Of course, there were and are also stronger alcoholic drinks on the market, depending on the colonial traditions of the different countries. In North Africa and in the Syro-Lebanese region, it is imported cognac or cognaclike brandies produced in these countries. In countries where the British were the colonial power, it is whiskey and gin, also either imported or locally produced. Normally the upper classes of both sexes consume these stronger drinks. For them it was and is modern, advanced, or enlightened to have a glass of scotch or a gin-lemon. But there are also some strong alcoholic drinks that are typical for the region. The most famous is a pastislike drink that is distilled one or two times from raisins, fresh grapes, or dried figs and flavored with aniseed. Like pastis, it turns cloudy white if mixed with water. Normally it is served very cold with ice, either already mixed with water or in two glasses, one with the drink and the other with water. Because of its color it is called "lion's milk." This drink, which is called *raki* in Turkey and *arrak* (sweat), can be found in Turkey and the countries of the Fertile Crescent. It is produced in private factories, but very often these places are state-owned. In North Africa there is an alcoholic drink made from figs that is called *boukha*, which is consumed pure.

In some parts of the Near and Middle East and North Africa, especially in Algeria and Tunisia in North Africa and in Turkey and Lebanon, there is also a modern production of wine. Wine production has a long tradition in the region, and one still finds traditional types of wine that often come from still existing Christian monasteries. These wines have a very sweet taste and quite a high percentage of alcohol. Today, especially in Turkey and Lebanon, remarkable qualities of red, rosé, and white wines are produced. These are consumed within the countries and exported only to a minor extent. The same can be said about the production of wine in Tunisia, which is mainly of the red kind. Algeria is the largest wine-producing country in the world. Most of the production is red wines, and most is exported, especially to France.

Since the beginning of the religious awakening of Muslims in the Near and Middle East and North Africa—called re-Islamization—the attitude of the majority of the Muslim population of the region toward any kind of alcohol has changed. Whereas the consumption of all kind of alcoholic drinks was accepted even by the pious with a forgiving smile, and foreigners were not hindered at all, now there is a strong taboo on alcohol. In political debates in Muslim states, the question of alcohol always plays a role. The Islamic character of a regime is seen also by its stance on alcohol. To appease an Islamist opposition, governments take prohibitional steps where it is possible, such as in the state-owned airlines. In countries that follow a radical Islamic ideology, prohibition is one of the propaganda signs by which the government shows its Islamic character.

Dairy

In a cuisine where milk and dairy products play an important role, it is normal that drinks are prepared also from it. Many kinds of drinks are made from yogurt. They have the advantage that they can be prepared quickly and without much work. Cool, refreshing, and healthful is *ayran*, a Turkish yogurt drink. The yogurt is beaten until soft, then water is added and beaten until well blended. Often it is salted and sprinkled with mint. *Ayran* is always served cool. Variations of this drink are seen in many countries. The variations depend on the type and preparation of yogurt; sometimes milk instead of water is added, or sugar instead of salt, and in Iran slices of cucumbers are added to the drink. These drinks are prepared at home, but very often one can buy them in fast-food restaurants. Sometimes street sellers prepare this yogurt drink in large pots and give it to the customers by scooping it into glasses that come directly from the kitchen of the house.

A very famous drink is called almond milk. Peeled almonds and powdered sugar are mixed and ground as finely as possible to get a paste. This is mixed with some milk and put aside. More milk is mixed with powdered sugar, and some orange-flower water is added. Then the mixture of almonds, sugar, and milk is put through a sieve. Almond milk is always served cool.

Hot drinks are also prepared with milk. On the Arab peninsula, one liter of milk, three teaspoons of black tea, cardamom, cinnamon, and saffron are boiled, then pushed through a sieve and served hot. Sugar can be added according to one's taste. Another hot milk drink is flavored with finely ground orchid root. In Turkey it is a typical winter drink, and is called *salep*. Milk and sugar are cooked slowly with orchid root until it cooks, and after that the heat is reduced until the mixture starts to thicken. Then it is served with a sprinkling of cinnamon. Orchid root is very expensive. Therefore, many people turn to instant mixtures that are now on the market. But specialists insist that the traditional way of preparing this drink is the best.

Sherbets

Water is the main ingredient of many traditional and modern drinks in the Near and Middle East and North Africa. They all could be categorized under the heading of *sherbet*. The word derives from the Arabic root for "drink." Sherbets are drinks made with water and fruit juices. Many of them can be found in every fast-food bar, train, or bus station in the Near and Middle East and North Africa, like the lemon sherbet—made of water, sugar, lemon juice, and the grated rind of some lemon fruits. This refreshing drink is often served with ice cubes. Sherbets are also made with cherries, apricots, mulberries, tamarind, pomegranates, hibiscus, and more. Drinks are made from dried fruit, such as apricots. In this case the dried fruit has to be soaked in water for some hours, than pushed through a sieve, before the cooled water is added. Normally it has to be put through a blender. Some people sweeten this drink with sugar or honey.

Other drinks include those that might seem a little bit strange for a Westerner. There is a drink prepared with roses. It is made from water, sugar, some lemon juice, and rose petals, or instead with rose water. There are some more complicated recipes for drinks like one that is called *jullab*, which means "rose water" but contains no roses at all. The jelly of grapes is dissolved in water, and raisins are ground with an electric mixer. Then a censer is filled with some frankincense and made to smoke. The censer is placed into a larger pot that must be covered immediately and kept covered for about ten minutes. Then the censer is removed, and the jelly water of the grapes and the raisins are put in the pot and covered again quickly. The grape-water mixture and raisins will absorb the smell of the frankincense after some minutes. Both are mixed carefully and poured into bottles. This unusual drink is served on ice and with some pistachios.

Another drink is *boza*, which can be found in different preparations in many countries of the Near and Middle East and North Africa. In Turkey it is made from fermented bulgur, and is normally commercially produced. It is a typical drink for winter. This drink is sold in the pudding shops, where they sell milk pudding, as a typical drink that comes with the main product of the shop. Bulgur and rice are cooked in a pan until they have become a pulp. The pulp is pushed through a sieve to get a smooth puree. The puree is put back into the pan with some added sugar. The quantity of sugar will have its influence on the degree of alcohol of the drink. Stirred continuously, it is brought to a boil and cooked for some minutes. Then it is poured into a bowl to let it cool. Yeast is blended with some of the puree and left to froth. This mixture is added to the rest of the puree and left to ferment at room temperature for some hours, or even up to two days. The duration depends on the degree of alcohol intended. After a time, bubbles will appear at the surface. This liquid is drunk with a little bit of cinnamon. In some cases groundnuts, hazelnuts, or pistachios are added or served separately. In Egypt a drink of this name is made from licorice. Licorice powder is put into a piece of cotton and soaked in water for two hours or more. To this strong, bittersweet liquid, more water should be added. It is a summer drink and said to be healthy for the stomach and res-piration. For people who are not accustomed to the taste, it is an unusual drink, and it is said that they try it only once.

Soft Drinks

Besides these traditional drinks, there are now many international soft drinks on the market in the Near and Middle East and North Africa. One can find Coca Cola as well as Pepsi, 7-Up, Sprite, and many others at least since the time of the Second World War. Generally they are produced in the region according to the recipes and instructions of the mother companies. Until recently it was fashionable to drink them. Customers of bazaar shops were offered these drinks instead of coffee or tea. From time to time there were problems for some of the companies because of the political situation. In the 1960s, the Organization of the Arab League attacked Coca Cola because the company did business with Israel. But there were other soft drinks of the same type, and after some years the ban on Coca Cola was lifted. The general attitude toward soft drinks of Western provenance remained the same. They were seen as a sign of modernity and open-mindedness. Only since the beginning of this century has there been a new attitude. Western drinks are attacked by religious and political authorities more successfully than in the 1960s. These drinks are seen now as foreign and as a kind of attack on the cultural and religious traditions of Muslim culture in general and Iranian or Arab culture specifically. Instead of Western products, now some new products are on the market that differ in some ways from the Western ones. One example is Meccah Cola, which is a soft drink that resembles in some ways the Western cola drinks but is said to be less sweet and therefore less nourishing that the Western types. Meccah Cola, was invented by a Muslim journalist in France and is now even exported to Muslim countries. In Turkey a very popular soft drink is called Cola Turca.

Teas

Other drinks are prepared with hot water. One can describe them as a kind of tea or infusion. In some cases drinking these infusions has a medical or ritual purpose. In Egypt, for example, cinnamon and ginger are cooked for some minutes with water, then almonds cut into pieces and sugar are added and cooked for some minutes more. This drink is served hot on special occasions, for example to guests who come to offer congratulations on the birth of a child. There is also an infusion of dried leaves and the blossoms of the linden tree, which is believed to be good for the digestive system and for colds. Another infusion is prepared by cooking the flowers of the hibiscus with water, sugar, and some lemon juice. It is drunk both hot and cold and is famous for its very red color. Nowadays there is a big trend, almost a craze, to prepare drinks from many other plants and fruit like chamomile, lemon, orange blossom, mint, rosemary, ash blossom, or wild sage. The main ingredients can be bought prepackaged in many modern and traditional shops in the region. Of course, the real aficionados maintain that only the infusions prepared with herbs or fruit that they have collected personally are the real thing. One of the most favored of these infusions of this kind is prepared with apples.

NOTES

1. Tadeusz Lewicki, *West African Food in the Middle Ages* (Cambridge: Cambridge University Press, 1974).

2. Elizabeth Fernea, *Guests of the Sheikh* (Garden City, NY: Doubleday, 1969).

3
Cooking and the Kitchen

As in many other cultures and civilizations, in the Near and Middle East and North Africa the kitchen is normally the realm of women. But one has to distinguish between the situation in a private household and the great kitchens of restaurants, hotels, and public kitchens, which have a long tradition in the region. The traditional Near and Middle Eastern and North African family is a social group of at least three generations. This family structure has greatly changed since the 1960s for several reasons. The most important of them is that there has been a continuous migration from the countryside to the great cities. The consequence of this was that the costs for rent and accommodation were continually increasing, and only the upper class could afford big apartments or houses for an extended family. Now, most families can be described as nuclear, with two generations living together. This has had consequences also for the culinary culture and cooking.

THE TRADITIONAL HOUSEHOLD

Starting with the extended family of the Near and Middle East and North Africa, which can be found even today in the countryside and in the traditional quarters of the big cities, one could say that there is a clear hierarchy concerning kitchen work. As the extended family consists of a father and mother, their married sons and their wives and children, and their unmarried sons and unmarried daughters, it is natural for there to be a constant discussion over who has to do what. Generally, women prepare and cook the food. The decision about who has to do what is made by the oldest woman. Her directives are based on various criteria. These can be very personal, such as whom she likes more or who has more or more beautiful children. And there are, perhaps, more rational arguments, like a special knowledge or competence of a certain female member of the household for a special task like the preparing of rice. For the more complicated or elaborate parts of the cooking or certain difficult dishes, there is often also a competition between the women of the household about who can do it better. Their status in the family depends not least on their ability the make good bread, roast a tasty lamb, or prepare a special dessert. In these households the younger women and the girls learn the art of cooking under the elders' supervision. Often they try certain dishes on their own, and one can be sure that an older women always pays attention to what the girls are doing and gives advice whenever it is necessary.

In this kind of family, there are always also a certain number of female servants who also do the more menial tasks, as do the young women and girls. At the same time, the older servants are greatly skilled in kitchen work and are respected for this ability. So, generally, one cannot say that certain work has to be done, for example, by a certain age group of women, but there is the rule that the more heavy work, such as fetching the water or bringing the fuel, has to be done by the younger women or even girls or by the younger or middle-aged servants. The more skilled tasks have to be done by the older women, whether they are members of the family or just servants. Very old women are exempted from kitchen work, but normally try to fulfill some light tasks. As young boys spend a lot of time with the women until puberty, they also gain certain knowledge of cooking. Many of them, living on their own as students or migrant workers in foreign countries, start to do their own cooking, relying on the practices they had observed during their boyhood.

MODERN FAMILIES: NEW WAYS TO LEARN COOKING

The way of teaching the tradition of cooking to the next generation is still practiced, but today, especially in urban areas, the nuclear family is the rule. So the chain of tradition is in danger. In the rich oil countries in the gulf area there is another problem: the women of the house often do not like to cook, as it is seen as beneath their social status. Instead, they have maids who come from countries such India, Pakistan, Bangladesh, or the Philippines, and who are often expert cooks. This means that many of the day-to-day foods these families eat are influenced by South Asian or Southeast Asian kitchens. This situation was seen by some officials of the gulf countries as a real danger to the cultural heritage of this region. So for some years there has been a tendency to reinvent the old recipes and adapt them to modern kitchen techniques. The growing awareness of the health aspects of cooking also plays an important part of the culinary politics of the Near and Middle East and North Africa.

The situation for families in Near and Middle Eastern and North African countries with a more modest income is not better somehow than that of the rich in regards to cooking. The mothers and daughters of normal middle-class urban families are forced to work outside the home. Some of these families have servants, but these are often only young girls from the village whose task it is to care for the toddlers, do the washing, and clean the apartment. Normally they have no great experience in cooking. In most modern households, between Morocco and Iran, the knowledge of cooking is not passed from mother to daughter anymore, so the way of learning how to cook has changed. Learning how to cook is done now, in some cases, in schools. Already in the elementary schools, for example in Egypt, children become acquainted with simple cooking techniques. This might include the baking of simple cakes and other easy recipes. Boys also participate. Some countries have cooking schools. Here young women learn to prepare simple and complicated recipes. They learn not only the art of cooking, but also all that is connected to the conducting of the whole household from cleaning or calculating the household costs to the preparation for big receptions. These schools are quite expensive; not every young woman can afford to attend. Consequently, since the 1950s, the number of cookbooks on the market in the Near and Middle East and North Africa has increased. Some of them are written by the teachers of the cooking and household schools. The female authors declare that these books have the function of introducing young working women to kitchen work, because they think that home cooking is more healthful and less expensive than eating out. By and by, cookbooks have become an important part of the book market.

Since the 1960s, one can observe that the general subjects of cookbooks develop according to the political or ideological situation of the region. Until the 1960s, the Middle Eastern cookbooks mirrored the general international cooking world, with a strong emphasis on French cuisine, which was the consequence of the great political impact of the West on the Middle East. With the rising nationalistic movements such as the Pan-Arabism in the 1960s in the Middle East, special Arab cookbooks were published. But these cookbooks did not distinguish between the many regional kitchens of the Arab world, and gave the impression that it was one tradition only. At the same time, Turkish cookbooks appeared on the market and tried to maintain the high standard of the Turkish cuisine. Also, in Iran comparable books were on the market.[1] From the 1980s onward, a strong regionalism could be observed in Arab cookbooks, when special books on Algerian, Moroccan, Lebanese, or Omani food were printed. This goes hand in hand with a growing consciousness of the regional particularities and even identities of the Middle East. Most of these books are successful. One book on the cooking of Saudi Arabia had several reprints within a year, and other books on the same subject followed shortly after the first publication. It is interesting that the approach of this first book was semischolarly. The editors interviewed old women about the foodways of their youth, and on this traditional basis developed new recipes.[2] In Turkish cookbooks, one can detect a tendency to reconstruct the imperial Ottoman cuisine, taking modern cooking techniques into account.

Nohutlu Pilav (Chickpea Rice) (Famous Medieval Turkish Dish)

- 1/2 cup (100 grams) chickpeas
- 1 cup (200 grams) long-grain rice
- 1 chopped onion
- 2 tbsp. clarified butter
- 2 1/2 cups (600 ml) water or chicken or beef broth
- salt and pepper
- chopped leek or spinach (for decoration)

Soak the chickpeas overnight and drain. Cook them in freshwater for about 45 min. until tender. Drain well. Soak rice if necessary. Heat the butter and let the onion soften in it. Stir the chickpeas and the drained rice. Pour in the broth, season with salt and pepper, and bring the liquid to a boil. Reduce the heat and let cook until almost all liquid has been absorbed. Remove the pan from the heat, cover with a dry dishtowel, and press the lid down tightly on top. Leave to steam for 20 min. Fluff with a fork, add the leeks or spinach, and serve.

Lamb *Tajine* with Plums and Honey (Moroccan)

- 1 lb. (500 grams) lamb stew meat, cut into cubes
- 1 chopped medium onion
- 2 crushed cloves of garlic

- 1/2 lb. (250 grams) small pitted plums
- 3 tsp. honey
- 1 tsp. orange-blossom water
- a handful of fresh coriander leaves
- 2 tsp. toasted sesame seeds
- salt and pepper
- 1 tsp. ginger
- 1 tsp. tarragon
- 1 tsp. cinnamon
- olive oil
- water

Heat the oil in a saucepan and add the lamb cubes, onions, coriander, garlic, salt, ginger, pepper, tarragon, cinnamon, and water. Cover the saucepan and bring to a boil, then lower the heat and simmer for about 1 hour until the lamb is tender. Add water if necessary. Stir in the plums and honey and continue cooking for another 20 min. Add the orange-blossom water and bring to boil. Place in a serving dish and sprinkle with toasted sesame seeds. Serve very hot.

The Israeli kitchen is a special topic. There is a discussion whether it is a Jewish or Israeli kitchen. A Jewish specialist on that question declares, "People often ask me if there is such a thing as Jewish food. Because these dishes [e.g., grape leaves, *sambusak, konafa,* and other Near and Middle Eastern and North African dishes] have such a powerful hold on the emotions of Jews, are so much part of the ancestral memories and so tied to their culture and identity, I believe that they should be considered Jewish."[3] The authors of an Israeli cookbook hold that "most of the food we eat in Israel is not indigenous to the Eastern Mediterranean, but is Israeli by virtue of the fact that it is grown, prepared and eaten here. However, an educated palate can easily identify the major influences at work in Israeli kitchens. There is a North African or Maghribi influence.... Other influences come from Eastern Europe, where Jews once flourished and prospered. Israel's Arab population has contributed yet other influences."[4] Still, the way of learning how to cook is very much influenced by the ways this was done in the countries where the different immigrant groups came from. Of course, it is also, like in the other countries of the Near and Middle East and North Africa, a sociological question, depending on traditions, social status, money, and so on.

Since the 1980s all cookbooks published in the Near and Middle East and North Africa come with more color photos of the ingredients and step-by-step illustrations of the different stages of the work preparation. As with Western publications, some of the modern Near and Middle Eastern and North African cookbooks are too bulky and perhaps too expensive to be used in a normal kitchen, so it is perhaps not misleading if one considers them to be coffee-table books. At the same time, there are also cookbooks on other cuisines on the Near and Middle Eastern and North African book market. Normally these are translations of international cookbooks with the same illustrations used in the English, French, German, or Arabic versions. All these books are an interesting and impressive sign of the new and renewed fascination of the middle class with regional food and cooking. Food magazines are also available in the book shops. In many cases the famous chefs of great hotels are the editors of these magazines, and they have titles like *al-chef Ramzi*, where *Ramzi* is the name of the director of a cooking department within a hotel school in Beirut, Lebanon. Often these magazines will have theme issues on special occasions or preparing for receptions, children's birthdays, or important religious feasts with special meals or dietetic rules. The periodicals are in general lavishly illustrated with many advertisements and product placements for food and drink, kitchen equipment, restaurants, cooking schools, and so on.

In addition, many of the Near and Middle Eastern and North African daily newspapers now have a regular food section, covering success stories of famous chefs who reveal some of their recipes. There may also be a reader section where readers' letters are answered. The number of articles on diet topics in these daily papers has increased in recent years as well. Generally the relationship between health and food is a hot topic in all printed media in the Middle East. And again, like in the Middle Ages, food, cooking, and eating have become important topics for conversations, especially among women but also among men. They compare restaurants or exchanges recipes or even a certain dish within the neighborhood. Of course, this has to be regarded as an upper- and middle-class phenomenon, specific to the affluent cities and countries of the region. Lower-middle-class and poor people cannot afford to buy expensive books and magazines, let alone reproduce the recipes that need, in many cases, costlier ingredients.

As nearly every family in the Near and Middle East and North Africa, at least in the cities, owns a TV set, cooking shows have become a way for less affluent women to learn about cooking. Now these shows are part of regular programming; especially those Arab or Iranian shows that are produced in Europe by Arab, Iranian, Turkish, or international companies and sent via satellite to the Near and Middle East and North Africa. Of the dozens of Middle Eastern satellite stations, nearly every one has such a program. Some of them are structured like those on Western programs, such as where a "cooking duel" takes place, where two chefs and two more or less famous helpers have to prepare a meal from ingredients that are bought in advance without any plan, but with a fixed maximum of money that can be spent. There is also a set time during which the cooking should be done. Often some practical jokes will surprise the protagonists and the onlookers. Another cooking show, called *Can't Cook Won't Cook,* was developed by the Dutch TV company Endemol. In each of the episodes two couples are invited into the studio to meet a famous chef for a fun lesson in cooking. One member of each couple cannot cook or does not like cooking. Part of the program is to find out why they either do not want to cook or cannot cook. Then the spectators in the studio can relax and have fun seeing how their loved ones attempt to cook a tasty dish. The results are often hilarious, and sometimes a disaster. At the end of the allotted time for cooking, the onlooking partners are blindfolded, and the chef feeds them with morsels from the two competing dishes. They vote on their favorite, and the winner gets a prize.

There are also programs that are designed especially for an overworked housewife with little time to do the cooking. For example, one program has a "dish of the day," where every day at 11:00 A.M. a more or less simple recipe is proposed and the preparation is demonstrated. The dish is chosen according to the season, so that one can buy ingredients for a reasonable price, or according to regular social and religious occasions. There are also regular programs starring a famous chef who demonstrates the wide range of cooking possibilities, from starters to desserts and cakes. In some programs two persons are giving the cooking instructions. In this case, often one of them is an elderly lady who does the main cooking, while the other, often a younger one with less expertise, is helping and asking questions about special ingredients or more complicated steps of the preparation. The two protagonists regularly change their outfits and hairstyles for every dish, while the kitchen is always the same. There is also constant background music. In contrast to the cooking game shows, this type of program has a clear pedagogical approach. Both persons address the onlookers directly and give a lot of advice on the correct techniques for and ways of preparing a good meal. At the end, often a general commentary on the recipe is given by the younger person.

Like in many cookbooks, some TV programs inform viewers about table decorations for everyday meals as well as for special occasions. They show how the different dishes, glasses, and cutlery are to be placed, which type of tablecloth is needed, and how it can be prepared. Many programs of this kind show the many possibilities by which table napkins can be folded. Major parts of the program also deal with flower arrangements for the table. In this part of the program, often very simple and practical techniques are demonstrated. These programs are interrupted regularly by commercials that advertise food and kitchen products. There are commercials for kitchen appliances as well as for food products such as milk, cheese, or cream. The regular program also has product placement for food or cooking products. Normally these are international products. The longer kitchen programs take about 45 minutes, whereas the dish of the day lasts only about 10 minutes. The longer programs can also be bought in a video form, so that a viewer can repeat a program. These videos also include the commercials. Some families in the Near and Middle East and North Africa own a complete set of cooking videos of a certain program, which they have bought on subscription. One may wonder whether these videos are really used regularly or if they have the same function as the coffee-table cookbooks and are played only very rarely.

There is yet another type of cooking video. It is produced by companies that want to promote certain cooking ingredients, such as vegetable oil. These programs do not appear in normal TV programming. They are sold very inexpensively in supermarkets. The cooking is shown as on the TV programs, but the product is very much the star of the show. At the end of the TV or video show, the recipes are displayed on the screen. In some cases the cook invites the viewers to ask for the written recipes. The kitchens shown in these programs have all modern equipment, and only the decoration makes it clear the population of which country is primarily addressed: there are typical bottles or bowls of a certain region, pictures, or cloth decoration. But all this is only the background of the show. Cooking is central.

Besides these cooking shows, cultural and historical culinary shows are broadcast. These tell about the origin of certain types of food or drink that were first used or invented in the Near and Middle Eastern and North African regions, such as coffee, dates, and oranges. The history of the diffusion of these food products worldwide is given, and the English, French, German, or Spanish versions of the names of these products are explained. These programs also function to enhance nationalistic feelings and pride of the cultural achievements of the region among the viewers. So, in these programs, politics are central, in the end.

PROFESSIONAL COOKS

As for professional cooks in the Near and Middle East and North Africa, one has to distinguish between cooks in big restaurants and hotel restaurants and the cooks of traditional fast-food shops on the streets of big Middle Eastern cities. Restaurant cooks in the region learn their art as an apprentice in the kitchen of a big restaurant. In some cases there are teaching programs, but in many others it is still training on the job. That means that normally boys, after finishing school at the age of 14 years, start as helpers in a restaurant kitchen and learn step-by-step cooking and organizing of a big kitchen for a greater number of customers. Understandably, the level of cooking competence in these cases is not very high, so in many Near and Middle Eastern and North African countries, schools for professional chefs have been established, generally within the program of big hotel schools. Female apprentices also begin their instruction there, but they are in the minority. The educational program has an international scope. The success of the programs is astonishing. Many of the alumni leave the region. As chefs often do, they move from job to job all around the world. One can find a Lebanese chef in an international hotel in New York as well as in Berlin. Interestingly, one can find alumni of these schools working as chefs in high-class Italian restaurants in western Europe.

The cooks who prepare food in bazaars and on the streets are, of course, of a different kind. Normally they offer only one or two dishes. Their knowledge is normally passed down from the older generation—from fathers and grandfathers who had also been cooks. This type of cook may have also been active in other occupations such as construction worker, watchman, or servant, and switches to selling food occasionally. Often the whole family, from the children to the grandparents, is involved in the business, but normally it is only the males of the family who are in contact with the customers. The women are busy preparing the initial steps of the preparation of the dish. As their cooking focuses on one or two recipes, the cooks have a solid knowledge about the way their product is accepted by customers. With a traditional product it is necessary to react to a change in the taste or modernize it in some situations. This is, of course, a complicated task, because their customers would eventually be irritated by any addition or change of the traditional recipe and the taste of the dish. The fast-food sellers particularly have to react to general changes in tastes and food habits.

KITCHENS

The Desert Kitchen

There are as many types of kitchen and kitchen utensils as there are culinary cultures in the Near and Middle East and North Africa.[5] Furthermore, kitchens are different in cities and villages and in cities in the affluent quarters and the poor quarters. In the compounds of the Middle Eastern peasants or in a bedouin camp, one can detect nothing that can be called a kitchen in the normal sense of the word. But, of course, there is a place where the cooking is done and where some kind of fireplace is installed. As the bedouin camp is moved from place to place in regular cycles, the place where cooking is done has to be moved now and then. So the kitchen utensils of nomads must be light, nonbulky, and of a strong constitution because of the constant packing and unpacking of these items.

The bedouin camp is generally separated into the men's part and the women's part. Both sections are separated by some cloth or curtain hanging on a line stretching through the tent. In the men's part, where guests are welcomed, one can often find a metal basin with a glowing fire for the preparation of coffee. Somewhere there is also storage for the cups and the sugar bowl. Often water is also available in a jar. So the coffee for a guest can be prepared without the appearance of a woman of the family. Often, especially in the tents of the important persons and families of a tribe, there is a big collection of the typical coffeepots and cans to make sure that the host will not be embarrassed by a greater number of unexpected guests. In the women's section one finds the kitchen utensils, mostly jars for the fetching of water, which is often the duty of the young girls, who sometimes have to walk long distances to get it. These jars were made of clay until the 1950s, so the task of carrying them from a spring or well to the family camp was hard and tiring work. When jars or bottles made of plastic were imported, they were preferred by the women. The jars are positioned in such a way that the wind could cool them, which means at the side of the tent, especially when this lateral part is opened. Jars made of clay can keep the water fresh, because very small quantities of water evaporate through the material and cool the jar. This cooling process is enhanced by the wind. Jars made of plastic do not produce this cooling effect, and the water gets warm and unpleasant after a short period of time. Therefore, many women pour the water that they have fetched in plastic jars into big jars made of clay to keep the water fresh.

Other utensils are large and small bowls made of metal or, today, plastic. They are used for the preparation of dishes as well as for the serving of the

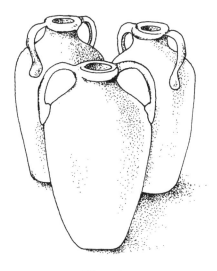

Water jars.

prepared food. There are also wooden plates that can be used as cutting boards for meat or vegetables. In some regions of the Near and Middle East and North Africa, like Morocco or Yemen, one can also find bowllike containers made from palm leaves or certain types of grass. These containers come in different sizes. Often they have a colorful decor, or a material of different color is used, so that they look nice and can be distinguished by their design. This design is traditional and transmitted from generation to generation in the family of the producer. Some of the weaving of these containers is twisted so densely that there is a proverb that says the containers can keep water. This may not be true, but vermin cannot get into the inner part of the container. Normally the container has a lid made of the same material and in the same technique. Sometimes the container and the lid are made in such a way that one can close the lower part with the upper one so that it needs some force to separate them, so no dirt or other unwelcome things can enter the inner part.

The work of cooking and preparing food is done mostly with the hands, and in some cases with knives or spoons of different size. Forks are used only rarely. Traditionally, eating is generally done with the right hand, so cutlery is not needed, and as the whole family eats from one big plate, no small plates for the individual eater are needed. The only heavy utensils of a bedouin kitchen are a stone mill for the grinding of grain and a mortar and pestle. The stone mill consists of two round stones, of which the upper has a handle. This is turned in a circular movement on the lower one. In some cases the two stones are connected by a tongue on the lower one and a hole in the upper one. The two stones are put together, and one can put the grain through the hole onto the lower stone and grind it. The other heavy equipment of the bedouin kitchen, the mortar and pestle, are also made of stone and/or metal. They are used to grind vegetables, meat, and other items.

Sometimes all these utensils are stored in chests or just in a sack. There are also the instruments used to process milk products. Every family owns the sack by which butter is made in a very tiring process. There are also the bowls for sour milk. Hanging from the ceiling of the tent or from a tent pole might be some nets made of palm leaves or the like. They contain foodstuffs such as vegetables, which cannot be reached in this position by vermin, which are everywhere. There is no need for items that could cool or preserve food. Meat is very rare and will be eaten immediately, and only dried ingredients are transported when the camp is moved.

For all bedouin kitchens, the fireplace is central. As the climate of the Middle Eastern deserts is normally dry, and rain is a gratefully received exception, the fireplace for cooking is situated near, but outside, the women's compartment. The fire is often lighted directly on the ground, and the pots are put directly into the fire or the hot ashes. Perhaps there are only some stones positioned in the glowing fire on which a pot is placed. Some nomad families also use a tripod from which the pot is hung over the fire. In any case, this type of cooking is not very effective, because only a small part of the heat produced by the fire will reach the cooking pot. But there is perhaps only one traditional solution for this technical problem, which is the digging of a cooking hole. Bedouins do this sometimes, but they prefer to find a natural shelter against the wind and try concentrate the heat of the fire this way. More effective is the cooking on the hot ashes. This cooking progresses, of course, quite slowly. But, as time does not play an important role in bedouin life, this does not matter too much. As nomads have no oven to bake bread, this is also done in the hot ashes. After it is baked, the loaves will be cleaned of the ashes and eaten. There is always the danger that the fire will get out of control and set the tent or the whole camp on fire, so the women are always very careful and watch the fire continuously. The other problem with this kind of open fire is that toddlers and other small children can get burned by falling into the fire or coming into contact with hot ashes. This type of cooking setup is typical for the nomadic life of bedouins who roam the deserts of Libya, Egypt, Syria, and Iraq. Generally, one could say that these bedouins are living a poor life and are often hungry.

Other people like to roam in the desert. On the Arab peninsula, a modern way of "bedouining" has developed. Since the beginning of the oil boom after 1973 in that region, rich Arabs from Saudi Arabia or the United Arab Emirates, for example, love to spend weekends and short holidays in the desert. The weight for transportation of the equipment of their tents is not an issue, as they have big cruiser cars that can carry what is needed for a nice time far from civilization. They have television sets to receive satellite programs, computer systems to connect with their business offices or the international stock exchange, and so on. But some practices, especially those related to food, are the same as those of the poor bedouins in other parts of the Middle East. First, the men's and women's parts of the tent are still separate. Today, often, two or more tents are erected, one for the men and the other for the women. The women's tent is where the cooking is done. Second, when eating, they still take their food by hand from one big plate. But now, much of the food is prepared by servants in the family kitchen in the city and brought to the desert camp. Of course, frozen food is also used. That means that one of the most important utensils of the modern way of bedouining is the refrigerator, which is normally installed in one of the cars. Water is also brought out from the city, so there is no need to camp near a natural water source. As the consumption of meat has increased on the Arab peninsula since the 1980s, rich "Arabs of the desert" are doing more grilling. Of course, electric grills are in use. But most bedouins of this type prefer charcoal grills, as they believe that the meat is more tasty, so charcoal has to be taken into the desert. Barbecuing techniques are different from Western ones, and special utensils have to be brought. Long skewers are needed to thread kebabs, bite-size pieces of meat, fish, chicken, or even vegetables. Minced meat is pressed onto oblong forms around flattened thin steel blades, which distribute the heat during cooking and prevent the meat from sliding off into the coal. As weight is not an issue, many transport heavy metal pots and clay jars. The clay jars are typically used to cook vegetables such as beans or to prepare eggs. This kind of living in the desert has a deeply nostalgic aspect. This also finds its expression in the ways food is prepared and consumed. Very typical is the roasting of a whole sheep, perhaps filled with rice. For that one needs a spit. Of course, now there are spits powered by a small electric motor.

The utmost in culinary nostalgia in this kind of desert life is a recipe for *shuwa*, which means "grilled." Traditionally this recipe is a specialty for the great Muslim feasts at the end of the holy month of Ramadan or the feast of pilgrimage. It is also prepared to celebrate a wedding, the birth of a firstborn son, a circumcision, or a peace treaty between hostile bedouin groups. Today it is done on many additional occasions, such as the opening of a big business building or the finishing of a complicated and important work, and even tourists will be treated by those who undertake an organized desert expedition of one or two days. For *shuwa*, a great fire pit must be dug in the ground. As the deserts on the Arab peninsula often have a hard and stony bed, this tiring work is done by servants. And in this case, pickaxes and spades become kinds of kitchen utensils. Additional stones are used to line the pit. Also, some kind of lid is prepared from metal or wood to cover the fire pit. A very hot fire is built then, using not only small and dry twigs and boughs, but also pieces of wood as big as can be found. Meanwhile, the meat is prepared. The skinned sheep or goat is left whole. It is basted with a liquid made of date pulp and often honey and lemons. Then it is salted and seasoned with a mixture of different spices such as cloves, cardamom, cumin, cinnamon, and others. Today, chilies, garlic, and ginger are also added. Then the meat is wrapped in banana leaves and securely sewn into sturdy sacks made of natural fiber. Special sacks woven from palm leaves for this purpose can be also bought at the local markets. Empty rice sacks and other such substitutes are often used in the same way. When the fire is really hot, the sack with the meat is dropped into the fire pit and covered immediately with the prepared lid or some stones. Then a thick layer of earth and gravel is added onto this lid. By this technique the fire is extinguished, but the heat is retained for a long period. The fire pit is left like that for 24 hours, and the meat cooks very slowly. Then the meat is taken out of the still-hot fire pit. The sack and the banana leaves are thrown away and the deliciously spicy, succulent roast is served hot on a very large communal plate, normally with rice and Arabic bread.

The Traditional Urban Kitchen

Near and Middle Eastern and North African cities can be distinguished by their size. There are the small rural cities with some thousand inhabitants and the big megalopolises like Cairo, Ankara, or Tehran with millions of inhabitants and millions more who commute in every day. The architectural features of rural cities and the traditional parts of the big cities have much in common. One can find two kinds of houses. The first one is a kind of compound. That means that the rooms of a single-story house are built around one or more courtyards of different sizes. If there are more courtyards, the kitchen can be found at a smaller one, often with a special entrance by which firewood, water, and large quantities of foodstuffs can be brought in. The kitchen rarely has a chimney, so the smoke of the fire can exit only through the door or a window, if there is one. Often there are also a fireplace and oven for baking bread in the courtyard. The oven is always outside the house. It is often built of clay and has a conic form. On the ground there is a hole where one can put the firewood into the oven. On top there is another hole through which the bread loaves are put into the oven. Among the utensils for making bread are a cushion by which the bread slices are stuck onto the side of the heated oven and a metal hook to take the baked bread out of the oven. In the courtyard one can find also water jars and a basin for cleaning pots and plates.

Sometimes one can find a clay construction that could be compared in its function with a sideboard in a Western kitchen. Often it is a round and about one meter high. It consists of two parts. The lower part is a support with several holes for storing kitchen utensils and dry foodstuffs. The upper part, with a larger diameter, is used for tasks such as cleaning vegetables. The side of this upper part flares outward so that small vermin cannot enter the upper part, but rather fall on the ground.

The courtyard is also the place where the firewood can be stored. The fireplace can be an open fire that is lit in an oven of clay with a hole on the ground for the fuel and one on top where a pot can be placed. In North African countries one can find a mobile fireplace, called a *qanun*. In classical Arabic, this word designates a metal basin in which a fire is made to warm up a room. In Morocco today it is a transportable item made of clay and fired by the potter. It has a round form and consists of a foot and an open upper part with sides. In the upper part, the fire is lighted. The *qanun* is covered by a simple mobile grid made of steel or iron. The *qanun* is used for cooking, baking, and grilling. A modern development in this *qanun* is a round construction consisting of a lower part made of metal with four feet and two or four handles. On the side there is an opening with a door, which is needed to light the fire and to fill with wood or charcoal. Immediately on the lower part the cooking pot is placed in a way that no heat can pass it. By this simple but original construction, the problem of an open fire, which loses more than two-thirds of the heat, is solved.

To get the fire going, several types of fans are used. The most simple one can consist of a large leaf of a banana tree. More often, one can find woven dried leaves attached to a handle. And in many Near and Middle Eastern and North African households, one can find a pair of bellows.

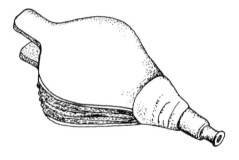

Bellows.

This can be very simple, often made of goat leather and wood; others are additionally decorated nicely, for example with little mirrors or small metal pieces.

Modern Kitchens

As it takes a lot of time to heat all these types of ovens so that cooking is possible, most kitchens, even the simple ones, nowadays have a modern cooking device. It can be a kind of a camping stove, called a *wapur* (from the French *vapeur*), often with only one flame, fueled by gas. This stove is small enough that it can be used easily inside the kitchen and in the courtyard. The *wapur* is always positioned on the ground, so that in case of an accident the damage will be minor. The cooking has to be done in a squatting position, which is quite tiring for the women, although they are used to it by long years of training. Sometimes women, especially the older ones, sit on a low stool. The simple kitchens usually have only one of these stoves. The women who do the cooking demonstrate a great competence in cooking more than one dish on one stove by changing the different pots continuously as the state of the dish requires. Traditionally, food is seldom served very hot in the Middle East, a fact that makes cooking with one flame less complicated.

Another item operated with gas is a burner with one flame only. This is used, especially in the Fertile Crescent, to burn the skin of eggplant for the preparation of the famous starter *baba ganush*, or *mutabbal*, which gets a delicious smoky taste.

Traditionally holes were dug into the ground to store vegetables, and in rare cases dried or smoked meat. Now, every kitchen has a refrigerator. Normally in the kitchen one can find a simple wood cupboard for storing various utensils. The lower part has a door or two; the upper part is open. In the lower, pots and plates are stored. On top, the housewife shows off some items such as glass or porcelain plates or cups, a doll, some photographs in a glass frame, artificial flowers, or other kinds of souvenirs. Kitchen utensils stored in the cupboard are bowls of unfired clay and also, sometimes, ceramics in different colors and designs. The latter ones are also used to prepare and store dairy products such as yogurt. The ceramics are usually green with dark arabesques or simple pictures of fish and other symbols that ward off the evil eye. There are also pots of various sizes, mainly bigger ones that can hold ten liters and more, normally made of cheap, thin metals, darkened by the long use on open fire. Normally there is one or more bigger knife that is used for various kinds of household and cooking work. A housewife may cut a small onion with this long knife—the only one she has. There are also spoons of various sizes for cooking and eating.

Beside the compound houses, one can find also traditional brick houses with several stories. The most famous are in Yemen and Hadramawt in the south of the Arab peninsula. These houses are normally inhabited by an extended family with their servants. Yemeni houses are famous for the *mafraj*, a top story with nicely decorated walls and windows, which is used as a kind of a salon for the men of the house, who have their khat (a mildly intoxicating herb) parties there.[6] The rooms for the storing of firewood and foodstuff are in the basement of the house. The kitchen is normally found on the ground floor and is equipped like those in the compound houses. With this setup, it is also possible to do the cooking outside.

In the big cities in the Middle East, four different types of quarters can be distinguished. First, there is the traditional business center, the bazaar. Normally people do not live here, but rather in the traditional living quarters adjacent to the bazaar. In the bazaar area one can find some small restaurants and a few bigger ones that have kitchens equipped according to the dishes they offer. So some only have facilities for grilling chicken or kebab, a refrigerator for cooling soft drinks, and a basin for water to wash the dishes or vegetables. Bigger restaurants in the bazaar area offer traditional food on a larger scale for tourist groups and groups of businessmen who are discussing new projects or old problems while eating. Sometimes in these restaurants, marriage feasts are held. These kitchens have big gas stoves and several grills, big refrigerators, and so on. As manual labor is very cheap in many traditional Near Eastern cities, kitchen gadgets are seldom seen. Even tiring work in the kitchen, such as the mincing of meat, is done by hand. In the modern business centers, one finds, of course, modern restaurants with Western-type kitchens.

The kitchen in the new and modern living quarters is situated away from the main entrance of the house, but with its own door to the outside, so that the housewife or the servants can come and go without being seen by an unexpected visitor. All that is needed in the kitchen can be brought in by this door. Normally the only cooking done outside is for grilled meat or vegetable kebabs. The kitchen will have an electric grill.

Modern Kitchen Tools

The most important item in the modern Middle Eastern kitchen is the gas stove. Normally it has four open flames, and sometimes even five or six. Now there are also gas stoves with a glass ceramic field. In this case there is still one open flame to burn, for example, the skin of eggplant. The stoves also have an oven as one would find in the West. Stoves are typically gas-fueled rather than electric. The reason is that in many parts of the Middle East, electricity is used only for the lights or TV set. Housewives feel more independent if they can use gas. The gas comes in gas canisters of various sizes, which normally last for one month. Often there is a second one in reserve. The canister can easily be connected with the stove, but this has to be done with care; otherwise it can lead to serious accidents. Therefore, many housewives prefer that the gas-canister supplier does it when he makes his regular stop. Trucks loaded with dozens of gas cylinders driving through the streets are a familiar sight. One can also see young boys with a sort of cart on which up to four cylinders can be placed. They deliver the canisters from small shops to the kitchens of the neighborhood and take the empty ones back to the shop to be refilled.

With the increasing use of frozen products, often ready-made meals, microwaves are common. Sometimes there is even more than one refrigerator. Some are just for food that needs little refrigeration, like vegetables. A second one is used for prepared food that needs a colder temperature. And there is, of course, a freezer. The modern houses in the Middle East normally have no cellar, so there is often an adjacent pantry. Often this room has no window, or the window is covered by a piece of cotton so that only some light can come in. Housewives know certain techniques to protect these foodstuffs from vermin or flies. Egyptian housewives, for example, put salt into their rice reserve to avoid ants. The food is stored in wood or laminate cupboards.

A typical modern kitchen will have cupboards and a sideboard. There is also a table and some chairs for preparing food. Among the utensils needed in a Middle Eastern kitchen are pans of different sizes, made of iron or tinned copper. As the normal burner is an open gas flame, iron is preferred. These pans are used for the frying of all kinds of vegetables and for minced meat. An ancient method of cooking meat, poultry, or even rice requires a heavy pan with a tight-fitting lid. At a certain point during cooking, the lid is sealed to the pan with a dough paste, which blocks any steam from escaping the pan. Traditionally, hot charcoal or hot water is placed on the concave lid of the pan so that the food is effectively heated from both sides.

Various kinds of sieves are also important. They can be of different sizes, but more important are the degrees of fineness. A colander is for the draining of salads and vegetables. The other type is a sieve with a fine net of cloth, metal, or plastic, for sieving flour and things like that; another type is needed for pushing through minced meat, to make it very fine and smooth. A more traditional sieve can be found in country kitchens. Normally it is round and deep and used for separating leaves and olives after the harvest. In an up-and-down movement, the olives are made to jump in the sieve and the leaves are driven by the wind while sand is falling through the sieve. After that the olives can be washed. The Arabic language has only one word for this type of utensil: *misfat*.

Various pots are made of iron, steel, tinned copper, and aluminum. Normally they are round. In many parts of the Middle East these pots, especially the smaller ones, have no handle and are easier to store. Only the biggest one of a set of pots has a handle that helps to move it around, especially when it is filled. All pots have a lid. Normally they are made with a groove so that they can be stacked when they are filled with food. Sometimes a metal clasp will hold the stacked pots together. This way up to three the pots can be transported without the risk of spilling. These pots are often nicely decorated in a special technique that is called *taw-shiring*, which means that wires of a different metal than that of the pot itself is hammered in arabesques onto the outer side of the pot. The lids can also be used as plates on the table. Of course, the person who does the cooking with these pots has to see the he or she does not get burned by the heated material.

Typical of the Middle Eastern kitchen are round, flat pots of varying sizes with a rim called a *siniyya*. Normally they are used to put cleaned vegetables or meat on or any other food that is being prepared. These special pots are normally not used on the stove. They are also used for serving greater quantities of food in the place of bowls. On a *siniyya*, of course, the cooked food will become cold more quickly than in a porcelain or ceramic bowl. A pot that is very typical for the North African cuisine is the *couscoussiere*, a French term. The *couscoussiere* consists of two pots of tinned copper, aluminum, or ceramic that sits one on top of the other. Both pots have two or four handles. The bottom pot is usually convex. The base of the pot on top has many holes like a sieve. The whole construction is covered by a lid. For cooking couscous, a fine cloth is spread onto the bottom of the upper pot. In the bottom pot a broth of vegetables, meat, and spices is cooked. The couscous grains are steamed by the cooking liquid from the bottom pot. There are also electric *couscoussieres*.

Another special cooking device of North Africa is the *tajine*, in which a dish of the same name is prepared and cooked. It consists of a round clay plate and a cylindrical, conic clay lid. (A metal *tajine* is normally a souvenir for tourists.) The *tajine* has no handles. Its lower part has a kind of a very flat foot so that the heat can be spread all over the plate. The conic lid allows steam to return to the food, so that the dish is rarely burned. *Tajines* differ in quality. Some simple ones have no decoration; elaborate ones might have traditional motifs such as against the evil eye. Because *tajines* break now and then, they are inexpensive. The price is one reason why Moroccan housewives prefer *tajines* to modern cooking pots; the other is that the slow cooking at a low temperature gives a special delicacy to the food.

Typical in the Turkish kitchen is a pot called a *güvec*. It is an earthenware pot used for cooking and serving vegetables, fish, and meat casseroles and stews. Traditionally the pot was buried in hot ashes of an open fire or an outdoor oven or kiln to cook. Another common item in the North African kitchen is a small, round, thin metal plate. It is used on both sides. On the turned-up bottom of the plate, very thin leaves of dough are produced by dotting the soft dough on the equally heated plate. The thin layers are used for the preparation of special cakes. The Tunisian *brik* (see chapter 2) is also made on this plate. Turned the other way, around with the small sides up, this plate is used to prepare the famous Moroccan *bstilla*, a dish made of puff pastry filled with pigeon meat.

In the eastern part of the Near East, a heavy cast-iron sheet that looks like a griddle is used for making of scones. It is used for preparing the kinds of bread that come from the Indian subcontinent, such as chapatis, rotis, and *parathas*, which are not only eaten by the Indian and Pakistani contract workers in Saudi Arabia and the United Arab Emirates, but also by the Arab population.

In kitchens of large households and in those of restaurants and fast-food shops, one can find another typical Middle Eastern kitchen device. It is the instrument that is used for the production of *döner-kebab* (or *shawarma* in Arabic). One can find *döner-kebabs* on the menu of restaurants of every kind. This famous dish has a relatively short history. According to Turkish traditions it was first produced about 170 years ago in Anatolia. To prepare good-quality *döner-kebab*, one needs several things. First, one needs a skewer that is more than one meter long, for the layers of marinated meat. The skewer is placed upright with a metal plate with its short sides positioned below to keep the fat and other liquids that drip down the structure during the grilling. Normally, the heat is electric or gas placed behind the meat as it constantly revolves on an electric motor. The Turkish word *döner* means "turn around." The parts of the meat that are ready for eating are cut by a swordlike knife and fall into a special small shovel that has a slightly indented side, so that the cook can bring it very near to the meat and nothing can fall down beside the shovel.

One kitchen utensil is the scraper used for the scraping of vegetables or fruit. The most common one has four sides for different kinds of slicing as well.

In the Middle East kitchen, minced meat plays an important role. Traditionally, mincing was tiring work. The meat was cut first in small cubes with a very sharp knife, and then minced until was soft. It was time consuming, and, especially during the hot summer, flies would land on the meat and one's hands and face. The flies could accidentally become part of the minced meat. So women in former times preferred to prepare recipes with this kind of meat in colder seasons, or to do the work early in the morning. Today an electric mincer is commonly used. Some housewives still use a mincing machine operated by hand, for economy or lack of electricity, but expert cooks who want perfect results are convinced that the electrically minced meat has too much liquidity, so that the kebabs formed from this meat will be too dry after frying or grilling. There have been debates on this in newspapers and in private conversations among housewives. At any rate, the more traditional machine operated by hand is the preferred method.

All kitchens have the traditional mortar and pestle, made of a heavy material like brass or porcelain. Sometimes the pestle is made of a very hard wood. These instruments are used to grind various nuts or herbs to prepare pastes or sauces. One can also find a small electric mill for grinding herbs, but one gets the impression that this electric mill is never used and is more for show. Housewives will explain that they use the electric mill only if they have to prepare great quantities, and that the mortar and pestle are easier cleaned than the electric mill. Those who have no electric mill say that results can be better controlled if the work is done by hand. More often used in the modern kitchens of the regions are kitchen aids such as hand blenders or mixers for the preparation of dough, pâté, or pulp. As tomatoes are today an often-used ingredient in the Near Eastern kitchen, a sievelike hand mill to prepare a tomato pulp and other vegetable pulps is a very common item.

Another item that is especially to be found in the cities of the region of the Fertile Crescent is a high-pressure steamer pot, used for the quick cooking of chickpeas for the hummus, one of the most important parts of the *mezze*, the selection of starters on the Middle Eastern table. There are big clay or wooden bowls that are used for the preparation of a bread dough, and there are plates of the same materials to produce couscous. In many regions one finds great bowls with a lid that are used for keeping bread. In Morocco these bread keepers are also made of wicker. In regions of the Near and Middle East and North Africa such as Iran, where the cooking of rice is considered an art, there are techniques that give the rice a texture that is thought to be perfect. The highest culinary quality of cooked rice is dryness. To reach this state, the boiled rice is put into a different pot after cooking. A kind of a round cushion is placed on the rice that is called *damkuni*. This cushion is made from the leaves of the raffia palm, a tree that grows everywhere in the gulf region of Iran and the eastern shores of the Arab peninsula. The cushion is completely covered with a sheet of cotton and put onto the steaming rice. The *damkuni* receives all the humidity from the rice. Although this technique is still used, some Iranian kitchens have an electric rice cooker that was developed in Japan especially for the Iranian household. As Iranians consider slightly burned rice on the bottom of the pot to be a delicacy, these rice cookers can even do this. Iranians find it very amusing that Japanese manufacturers have developed this rice cooker especially for their taste.

Near and Middle Eastern and North African cuisine has deep-fried dishes. North Africa has fritters or "sponges," and on the eastern shores of the Arab peninsula and in Iran, different kinds of deep fried dishes are popular. The North African type of fritters are made in large, round iron pots and taken out of the hot oil, sometimes with a stick or a spoon. In the east of the region there is a cast-iron pot for deep frying that looks like a Chinese wok but is heavier and deeper.

A specialized item in the kitchen of the eastern shores of the Arab peninsula is a pot from India for making ice cream. The technique predates refrigerators. A mixture of milk, rice flour, sugar, almonds, double cream, rose water, and pistachio nuts is poured into one or more cone-shaped aluminum cases with a screw-on lid. These are then placed in a large earthenware pot that is full of ice and salt. The pot is then slowly rotated for smooth and creamy ice cream.

Even a very expert housewife occasionally needs to measure ingredients, so measuring instruments of different types can be found in the Near and Middle Eastern and North African kitchen. There are more and less complicated scales and graduated beakers or pots.

Of course, every modern Near and Middle Eastern and North African kitchen has several smaller utensils. The types, number, and quality depend on the economic and social situation of the household. The simple kitchens of bedouins and poorer village families have only a few instruments needed for cooking and eating. Some spoons and knives will do. The housewives will also improvise with other things. So they will take a stick found on the way to stir a soup or a stew. The modern middle class in the Near and Middle East and North Africa normally has a complete set of spoons and knives. Most households have a tablespoon; smaller ones are not common in the kitchens, although they are used for sugaring tea. There are also long, big spoons for serving stews and soups. There are also big spoons with several holes, which are used to take meat or vegetables out of a broth. And to finish, one can find also several wooden cooking spoons in different sizes.

It is remarkable that forks are not mentioned in the cooking books as necessary for a Near and Middle Eastern and North African kitchen. Of course, there is always the question of which of the many instruments are in fact used and which are just lying in the cupboard. A long knife is very important. It is used for preparing vegetables, meat, and fish. The backside of such a knife is also used to scale fish. There is also a small knife, and to mince meat or vegetables such as spinach, a chopping knife with two handles is needed. Very typical for the Near Eastern kitchen is the vegetable reamer, which is essential for hollowing out eggplant, zucchini, carrots, or potatoes. In traditional kitchens one can still find big, heavy knives or choppers for cutting whole animals such as a sheep or goat. But, as today housewives often buy their meat in a supermarket as needed for one meal, these heavy knives often play only a decorative part in the kitchen. Kitchen scissors are often used for cutting vegetables, cleaning fish, or opening plastic bags of frozen products.

Most Near and Middle Eastern and North African kitchens have several skewers of different size and form. Normally they are made of steel. Some are thin, like needles, and have one handle, normally made of wood. They are used for grilling morsels of meat or vegetables like onions and peppers. If these pieces are very small, skewers made of wood are also used. They are usually thrown away after one or two uses, because the wood cannot be cleaned like metal skewers. The other type is a blade with a handle used to grill minced meat. As the grilling process is very short, the handle will not become too hot.

Many instruments in the kitchen are needed for the preparation of bread and cakes. Often the bread is shaped by hand, and the housewives have an astonishing technique to shape it into a round form in a turning motion. But for cakes, the dough is flattened in the Near and Middle East and North Africa by a wood or plastic rolling pin. This rolling pin normally has two handles. But there is also a smaller one that is called in Arabic by a word that derives from the Arabic word for "arrow." It is made of wood or plastic and has a cylindrical form with a very small diameter.

Nearly every traditional and modern Near and Middle Eastern and North African kitchen has brass coffeepots for preparing Arab or Turkish coffee. Expensive pots may be engraved. These pots have a small middle portion, and opposite the long spout is a handle. The conic lid of the pot may end in a metal knob. These pots come in different sizes. There are smaller ones for only 2 or 4 little cups of coffee, but also larger ones for 10 cups or more. Often these coffeepots are lined up in a cupboard. Arab coffee is bitter, and one drinks only a sip. The other type of coffeepot that is often used has a long handle, so that it can be put directly on the flame. It is typically made of tin-lined brass, but cheaper ones are made from aluminum. The form is slightly conic. Some of the more expensive pots of this type are decorated with a simple design. The long handle has engravings. This pot is needed to prepare the so-called Turkish coffee, which is sweeter than the Arab coffee. Of course, one can find also a coffee mill for grinding the coffee beans and spices. These are usually electric-powered, but one can still find manual mills.

An important part of every kitchen is, of course, the set of things needed for serving the food. In traditional households, there are few serving plates. On many occasions everybody eats from one big plate that is put in the center. In the times of the bedouin groups roaming through the desert, this plate was made of leather, which was easily transported and compact. In traditional homes today these plates are made of tinned copper or other metals. Normally they have two or four handles. Some of these plates, which are also called *siniyya*, are big enough to serve a whole sheep with vegetables and rice. A big *siniyya* is, of course, needed only on rare occasions. As not every family has the means to buy one, it can be rented, for example, from the traditional bazaars of Fez in Morocco or Mosul in Iraq. Modern middle-class households have all the plates and bowls that are needed to entertain a number of guests or a big family. This tableware is normally made of porcelain, which also has a long tradition in the Near and Middle East and North Africa. Since pre-Islamic times, porcelain has been imported from China. Of course, one can find famous European brands, but the Chinese porcelain is still much sought after in many regions of the Near and Middle Eastern and North African world.

For drinking, different goblets, cups, small pots, and the like are produced of various materials. Glass has a long tradition in the Near and Middle East and North Africa. Even today (for example, in Jordan), local producers of drinking glasses sell their goods. These glasses are generally colored and resemble the style of those found in archaeological sites from Roman times. Very expensive glasses have engraved designs. For ages, these glasses have been decorated with designs in many different colors and even with small pictures of architectural sites, landscapes, and persons. In the rich oil countries of the gulf and elsewhere, glasses with inlays of gold foil in many decorative forms can be seen. There are also simple goblets made of earthenware, often with a handle. The number and types of glasses are few. As alcoholic drinks are taboo, there is no need to have glasses for wine, sherry, or beer. In some gulf countries, a sort of milk cult has developed where one drinks different kinds of animals' milk during a meal. Special glasses for the different kinds of milk have only now been available.

Cutlery sets consisting of knives, forks, and spoons were only recently found in the traditional Near and Middle Eastern and North African house. The most important instrument for eating was the spoon. It has a long tradition in the Near and Middle East and North Africa, since at least the time of the Abbasid caliphate (750–1258). There was even something like a spoon cult. Well-to-do people always used several spoons during the meal and changed for each dish. Nowadays, spoons are of course used to eat soups and other liquid dishes. For the other food, hands are used, mainly the right one. Bread pieces are used as a tool to take bits of hot dishes. Knives are also used rarely, because the meat is often served in small pieces or bigger chunks, or whole animals like chicken are separated with both hands and eaten directly. Modern Near and Middle Eastern and North African families still love to eat with their hands, especially when they are having a meal outdoors. But at home, middle-class and upper-middle-class households have several sets of cutlery with knives, forks, and spoons of different sizes. One can imagine that the whole set is not used for everyday meals, but only on special occasions such as weddings, circumcisions, anniversaries, or the main religious feasts when the family has to show their taste and refinement for guests or extended family. These households also own sets of assorted plates, bowls, and dishes. Compared with the normal Western household, they have many more small plates and dishes. This is because of the number of hot and cold starters. Often the *mezze*, the famous Middle Eastern selection of starters, consists of a dozen or more small dishes.

In middle-class households, tablecloths also play an important role. Traditionally, embroidery was an important task of women in the Near and Middle East and North Africa. Beside the preparation of food, all kinds of needlework were their most important activity. Like the cooking, girls learned from their mothers or other elder women of the household the different handicraft techniques by observing and imitating. In some countries, for years, the only way for housebound women to make some money for themselves was to sell traditionally embroidered napkins and such at the market. As a consequence, there is always a great interest in tablecloths among Near and Middle Eastern and North African women. Textiles are one of the general topics of conversation during women's tea parties and other occasions. During visits, it is common for a housewife to show some of her treasures to her female visitor. On special occasions, an expensive tablecloth will be noticed by the guests.

Since about the 1980s flowers have played a role in the decoration of the table. But this is still not common. Although there is also a long tradition of flowers in Middle Eastern culture—think only of the age of tulips in the Ottoman empire—very few flowers are generally known. Centerpieces are completely unknown. This is again surprising because of the tradition of decorating a table with small figures, animals, or plants was known in the Near and Middle East and North Africa during the Middle Ages. Often these figures were made of sugar and eaten at the end of the meal. From the Near Middle East this practice came to the northern European capitals, where the figures were made of more durable material, because sugar was much too expensive. This tradition in the Middle East has fallen into oblivion, but perhaps it will be reinvented in the near future by some creative chefs or TV producers.

NOTES

1. Bert Fragner, "Social Reality and Culinary Fiction: The Perspective of Cookbooks from Iran and Central Asia," in *Culinary Cultures of the Middle East*, ed. Sami Zubaida and Richard Tapper (London: Tauris, 1994), 63–71.

2. Peter Heine, "The Revival of Traditional Cooking in Modern Arab Cookbooks," in *Culinary Cultures of the Middle East,* ed. Sami Zubaida and Richard Tapper (London: Tauris, 1994), 143–52.

3. Claudia Roden, "Jewish Food in the Middle East," in *Culinary Cultures of the Middle East,* ed. Sami Zubaida and Richard Tapper (London: Tauris, 1994), 153–58.

4. Avi Ganor and Ron Maiberg, *Taste of Israel: A Mediterranean Feast* (Bnei Brak, Israel: Steimatzky, 1990), 14.

5. The following description of kitchen utensils is based on the introductions in a number of modern Middle Eastern cookbooks, especially Zubaida Mausili, *Min fann al-tabkh al-Sa'udi* (Jiddah: Dar al-'ilm 990); Rabiha Ahmad Hafidh, *Usul al-Tabkh al-sa'udi wa-l-sharqi* (Al-Riyad: Maktabat 1412 H.); Fatua Benkirane, *al-Tabkh al-maghribi al-mu'asir* (Paris: Soche Press 1985); Robert Carriere, *The Taste of Morocco* (London: Century Hutchinson, 1987); Nevin Halici, *Turkish Cookbook* (London: al-Kharijí 1987).

6. Armin Schopen, *Das Qat. Geschichte und Gebrauch des Genussmussitels Catha edulis Forsk. in der Arabischen Republik Jemen* (Wiesbaden: Franz Steiner Verlag, 1978).

4

Typical Meals

The meals of an ordinary Near and Middle Eastern and North African family differ according to geographical region, economic power, social status, and religious devotion. Peasants and urbanites have different rhythms in their eating habits. People in northern Iran have different kinds of food than do nomads of the Sahara. Taxi drivers in Cairo or Istanbul have many snacks during the course of the day, whereas a trader in the bazaar of Aleppo in Syria drinks many glasses of sweetened tea. Shiite Muslims avoid certain types of fish or rabbit, which are eaten by Sunnis. Christians eat pork, which Jews never do.

BREAKFAST

In many Near and Middle Eastern and North African households, mealtimes depend on the daily routine of children. Those members of the household who work outside often leave the house early in the morning, just after having finished a cup of coffee or tea. Especially in the cities, they prefer to reach their place of work while it is still cool, or at least not too hot in the streets. The pavement is wet down by the shopkeepers, which freshens the air a bit. When the number of cars increases and the all-day traffic jam starts, children and young persons zigzag through the lines of standing cars and offer early-morning snacks to the drivers. Others have established their short-lived shops on the sidewalks of the streets and use chains, meant to keep the pedestrians from crossing the street at random, to hang thin bread loaves on. Normally these snacks are sesame bread rings that can be found all over the Near and Middle East and North Africa and other kinds of sweet or salty types of small bread products. They also offer sandwiches, normally with salad, tomatoes, and cheese perked up with some hot spices. In the Fertile Crescent and Turkish cities, one can also find sandwiches with slices of *bastirma*. This is an Armenian specialty. It is a cured fillet of veal encased in a thick, dark-red paste made from, among other things, ground fenugreek, cumin, red pepper, and garlic. It varies from region to region, and every butcher has his own recipe for it. Other sandwiches have a paste of crushed olives. This traditional fruit of the Mediterranean and the Middle East is also offered in its many varieties and normally sprinkled with some spices as part of a morning snack.

Street peddlers also sell other light snacks in the morning. Some sell thick slices of carrots, kept fresh with water, or long slices of cucumbers, according to the season, while still others offer single stalks of silver beets and other kinds of green vegetables. Some peddlers sell fruit, usually apples during the season, but also oranges and different kinds of plums. In the hot days of summer, sellers of the many kinds of melons find thankful customers, even in the morning. Others sell sweets, either cakes or bonbons and the like. Those drivers who have to fight their way through the traffic calm themselves down not only by chewing gums, but more often by chewing on various nuts and seeds, which are also offered along the main roads. Pistachios, sesame seeds, cucumber seeds, and many others are eaten, and the shells are thrown or spit out of the car's window. Bus stops, especially the central bus stations of the cities, are also targets of the many food peddlers. Here they even offer hot snacks and tea or coffee as well as many kinds of local or imported soft drinks. In winter, typical soups of the season are offered. In Iran, for example, soup made of sheep's head is sold to the early workers in the bazaar area.

For those members of the family who stay at home or leave the house later, and for the children who go to school, normally there is a more quiet breakfast, but it is also quite early. Generally people in the hot climate of the Near and Middle East and North Africa get up early, especially in summertime, to take advantage of the relatively cooler period of the day for menial and more tiring work. School starts early in the morning. The breakfast generally consists of bread; cheese; yogurt; marmalade or jam; and raw vegetables such as carrots, cucumbers, and olives. Meat products like sausages are rare. Often eggs are served, boiled, fried, or scrambled. But there are many other intriguing combinations; one can prepare a kind of scrambled eggs and add yogurt to it while still cooking, or instead add wine vinegar or pomegranate syrup, or a mixture of water and sumac. On special occasions pancakes or crepes are prepared, or perhaps an omelet with parsley and pine nuts. In many cases the breakfast consists only of the leftovers of the last evening meal. In the hot summer, fresh fruit is served is the morning. It can be an apple, some oranges, or slices of melons, especially the big red watermelons, which are at the same time satiating and thirst quenching and well worth the money. For a short time during their season, fresh green or blue figs are also part of the summer breakfast. In autumn, branches of yellow dates appear on the breakfast table. They are eaten just as they come or in combination with soft white cheese. During winter and early spring, traditionally, there are dried figs and dried dates on the table. Today oranges are available nearly all year at a reasonable price, so that one can always have them at breakfast. In the modern parts of the big cities, many kinds of fruit are offered outside the natural season. But the majority of the population cannot afford to buy these luxury food items.

Today there is a strong tendency to adopt Western ways of breakfast, especially in the big cities, so one can find a continental breakfast with croissants or breakfast rolls. The normal drink in the morning is black tea with sugar. In some countries, where the British influence is strong, there is also tea with milk. Nowadays one is also used to instant coffee. Orange juice and other fruit juices are also on many breakfast tables, but this is a more recent tradition. Children get milk, and water is also a normal drink in the morning.

In some parts of the Middle East, like Lebanon or Turkey, it is typical to combine soft cheese and jam for breakfast. And, indeed, the combination of the lightly sour cheese with the sweetness of jam makes an interesting culinary experience for a newcomer to the Middle Eastern cuisine. For those eaters who are used to this sensation, it still has the effect of waking one up. The jam itself is a newcomer to Near and Middle Eastern and North African cuisine. Traditionally, fruits are consumed fresh or dried, and for a long time sugar was an expensive ingredient, so that not everybody could afford to make jams. But the Turkish housewives especially know some very original ways of making jam, and have a long tradition, whereas in other regions with an abundance of fruit the preparation of jams and marmalades was only introduced during colonial times, in most cases from England and France. Now small and big factories for the production of jam can be found in many countries, and the taste of these products has been standardized.

Still, some housewives make their own jam, and the renaissance of traditional cooking has among its consequences that these old recipes are

Woman pouring tea, near Matmata, Tunisia. ©
TRIP/H. Rogers.

found and reinvented. There is, for example, the exquisite rose-petal jam,
perfumed and runny with the smell of the petals of old garden roses. Although the preparation is quite simple, the collection of the rose petals
takes time and cannot be done by machines and is, therefore, too expensive for mass production. For this jam, the white ends of red or rosé petals
of roses have to be cut off. Then the petals must be rinsed and dried well.
The petals are put into a pot with water and brought to a boil. Then a
sieve is put on a bowl, and water and rose petals are thrown into the sieve.
The petals are set aside while the water is returned to the pot. The liquid
is brought back to boiling while sugar is added. Then the heat is reduced
and the liquid simmers for 10 minutes. Then lemon juice and the rose petals are added and left simmering for another 15 minutes. One can also buy
caramelized rose petals in some places in the great bazaars. These petals
can be added also. The pot with this delicate-smelling liquid is left to cool
and is then spooned into sterilized jars.

Another interesting jam is made of dried figs. For this, sugar and water are put into a pot and brought to a boil. Then the heat is reduced, and dried figs and lemon juice are added and simmered until the figs are soft and the syrup thickens. Then pine nuts can be added (some housewives also add cinnamon). The syrup, at the end, is spooned into sterilized jars.

Jams are also made from vegetables, like an eggplant jam that is made in the Turkish region of Antaliya. This tastes like a jam of bananas or a carrot jam that is known on the Arab peninsula. For this jam, carrots are peeled, washed, and ground and put into a pot; then sugar is added and the mixture is left for two hours. Then water is poured onto this mixture of carrots and sugar and all is cooked while stirring continuously until the sugar has dissolved and the carrots have become soft. Lemon juice is added and the mixture is put into sterilized jars.

Ful Mudammas (Egyptian Daily Dish)

- 1 cup dried fava beans
- 4 tbsp. fresh lemon juice
- 2–5 cloves of garlic, crushed
- 2 tbsp. chopped fresh coriander leaves
- 4 tbsp. olive oil
- salt and pepper
- cumin
- ground coriander
- hard-boiled eggs (if desired)

Soak the beans overnight, drain them, put them in a pot, and cover with water; cover the pot and cook over medium heat for about an hour until the beans are tender. Add water if necessary. Drain the beans and put into a mixing bowl. Add 2 tbsp. of olive oil, salt, pepper, ground coriander, cumin, lemon, and garlic, and mix until the beans are slightly crushed. Put the mixture into different bowls or plates and sprinkle with olive oil and coriander leaves.

Since the 1980s or so, there has been a change in food that is served for breakfast. In some countries (Egypt, for instance), it was customary to have at least one warm dish in the morning. It is called *ful mudammas*—a meatless stew made of brown or fava beans. As it was cooked in former times in the dying fire during the night, it was a natural dish for the breakfast. After all, it is a simple recipe. One needs brown beans and water, which are cooked on a low fire for at least six hours. Then part of the beans is mashed and put back with the rest. Before serving, crushed cloves of garlic, fresh lemon juice, cumin, parsley, olive oil, salt, pepper, and perhaps chopped green chili pepper and chopped tomatoes are added. Often eggs are put on the top. Experienced housewives put the eggs on the beans at the beginning of the cooking process, so that the eggs will, by the slow cooking, have a very special consistency. In the popular quarters of cities like Cairo, in the morning one can see scenes like that described by an anthropologist: "Small children flutter sleepily through the streets, unkempt cherubs in their floor-length gowns, commissioned to fill their enameled bowls with foul beans sold out of great round copper and brass pots that have simmered continuously throughout the night. Accidents are common as children teeter home through the uneven dirt streets with the steaming bowls; wails of anticipation of the smacks that await them at home rise in the morning air to produce the first real cacophony of the day."[1] Of course, there is some variation in the preparation of *ful mudammas* in various regions of the Near Middle East. For instance, in the Palestinian version, chickpeas also are added. In other parts of the Near and Middle East and North Africa, especially in North Africa, this dish is unknown. Still, there is a tradition of eating warm or hot dishes at breakfast in some regions. This continues until today, when warm pancakes with jam are prepared.

Today, dishes are served that are more typical for a lunch or supper. These are the famous cold starters, like chickpea or eggplant dips. A modern part of the breakfast is that fried eggs are sprinkled with some already-fried minced meat. This is a variation of the western ham-and-egg dish for all those people who have to avoid ham for religious reasons.

Children going to school and persons working out of the house often have a snack in the late morning. This is understandable if one considers that breakfast is eaten quite early in the morning. This snack is prepared for them by their mothers or other older females of the household. It may be a fruit such as an apple or some dates, a sandwich, or just a piece of dry bread, according to the means of the family. Some children get money from their mothers to buy a sandwich or pastry from peddlers flocking around the schools at the time of a longer break between the lessons. Others offer fruit such as melons or ice cream. Small shops or persons who sell soft drinks can also be found around the school buildings. Sometimes children take another snack after school, before starting to walk home, which can take awhile, as there is not public transport or it is too expensive. People at work also have snacks in the late morning, normally sandwiches or pastries. These are often also offered by peddlers who roam the business areas of the cities. There is a long tradition of this in the Near and Middle East and North Africa that goes back to the Middle Ages. Today there are also pizza deliveries at the disposal of working people. Many of workers drink some glasses of tea sweetened by some sugar. This dampens the appetite, so not all of them eat solid food at the second meal of the day.

LUNCH

When children return home after school and the grown-ups are still at work, there will be a light lunch for those in the house. It may consist of bread and soft white cheese, perhaps a soup, and some cooked vegetables. Often it is potatoes with turnips and tomatoes in a little broth made from chicken, veal, or lamb with very little meat. Occasionally it may only be a cake or some fruit. If the complete family is at home, the lunch will consist of more and more solid food. This lunch will normally take place in the early afternoon when the heat of the sun has subsided. If there are children who have the afternoon shift at school, lunch is timed so that they can be in time for school. That means that lunch is a little bit earlier than normal. Often this meal is prepared only for the children.

There is a clear distinction between the lunch habits of people living on the countryside or in small cities and those of the megalopolises. As commuting to work in cities such as Cairo or Tehran takes a lot of time, many people stay at work and return home only after they have finished their job. Depending on their financial situation, they will have a light lunch in a modern restaurant, consisting normally of one dish and a coffee afterward.

Those workers who cannot spent the money for a lunch bring something from home—a sandwich or bread, a melon or banana—while still others stay without food and smoke a cigarette to deaden the hunger. In smaller cities, even if they are of a major political importance (such as the capitals of the Gulf Emirates or Muscat, the northern capital of the Sultanate of Oman), people in most cases return home for lunch, and shops and offices will be closed until five in the afternoon. People eat their lunch at home and have a siesta after that before returning to their place of work, where they stay until eight or nine in the evening. In families who are eating together, this lunch can be described as a lighter meal compared with those eaten later. These dishes are not always specially cooked for the lunch, but can be leftovers. Depending on the region, there may be bread or rice on the table, cooked vegetables of the season, a little meat or fish, and a variety of fruit. The paucity of the dishes is understandable, because the heat in many regions during more than half of the year reduces the appetite.

More important is the need for drinks. So on the lunch table there is always water, often cooled with ice. Near and Middle Easterners and North Africans of all classes know about the importance of the intake of a sufficient quantity of liquids, and they know that water is the best for that. People might drink half a liter of water or more at once. Often there are also soft drinks on the table. But generally it is only one small bottle of a cola or anything else of that kind that is there for every person. The paucity is for two reasons. For many families, soft drinks are quite expensive, while water is provided at low costs. And commercial soft drinks, with their high percentage of sugar, are not always thirst quenching. Besides water, there are some yogurt drinks that have a long tradition of quenching thirst. It may be a mixture of yogurt or sour milk with water. The Turkish *ayran* and the Iraqi *laban* are famous; often salt is added to this liquid, which is also important because of the high quantities of salt the body is losing by sweat. So normally the lunch is a quick and less-important routine. It has never been the one and only occasion when the whole family comes together, and this is so until today. So the change in the economic situation with the commuting of workers from one place to the other has not brought a basic difference in the kind of food that is consumed today at lunchtime in the Near and Middle East and North Africa. Only on special occasions—religious festivals or private feasts, such as circumcisions or marriages—does the lunch last longer and become more elaborate, with a longer preparation of the many different dishes.

The evening meal itself, of course, differs from region to region and according to the various social classes. In big, traditional families, the male members of the family eat alone in a separate room, which the women enter only to bring the food and take the empty plates away. The males can participate in this group of eaters from an age where they are able to take the food by themselves and do not spoil the meal by their behavior. The women normally eat in the kitchen, often before the men are starting their meal. It is more informal. Often they eat while cooking. That means that the women eat from this dish and that, just as it comes. If there are more women working in the kitchen, they take turns filling it with food and eating alone, while the others are still working or looking after the pots. In other cases they eat when the men have finished with their meal and before cleaning up in the kitchen. Nutritional anthropologists have observed that the women see to it that the men, especially the younger sons, receive better food. That does not mean that the female members of the family have a lower intake of calories. It may even be higher, if one

Traditional meal in a Saudi home. © TRIP/
TRIP.

counts it all over the day. But the more tasty pieces of meat, more fresh
vegetables, or sweeter fruit is given to the males.

In modern families, men and women eat in the same room and at the
same time. But, of course, women have to get up and interrupt their meal
to work on the next course, bring the bowls, remove the empty plates, and
so on. In nearly all Near and Middle Eastern and North African households, a TV set is running while everybody is eating, but nobody listens
attentively to the program.

The number and quality of dishes for the main meal of the day stand,
of course, in a relation to the economic situation of the family. Another
important aspect is the region. In most parts of the Arab world, as well as
in Turkey, bread is an important food for the main meal. Without bread,
in many regions the meal is considered incomplete, although there may
be a great variety of dishes offered. That means that rice, potatoes, or

noodles are not seen to be as nutritious as bread. In Iran, bread is also important, but rice has the role that bread has in some parts of the Arab world. Vegetable use also depends on the region. In those parts of the Near and Middle East and North Africa where the climate does not allow certain vegetables or fruit to be grown, there may be imports from other regions; but, as these are more expensive, only a few buy them. Generally, meat is not a main part of the meal. This is because of several reasons. The first is that meat is expensive. Sheep and goats, as well as chickens in traditional families, are not only raised because of the meat, but because of the milk or eggs they produce, so in many cases they are slaughtered only when their productivity in this respect is reduced. In that case, the meat used in the kitchen is old and tough, so it is not a real pleasure to eat it. The consequence is that a certain number of recipes use minced meat, which is easier to eat and more quickly fried or grilled. That is also an advantage for fuel economy. Minced-meat dishes of this kind also have one more advantage. They can be mixed with vegetables, rice, or wheat products, so that the eater has the impression of eating more meat than he in fact does.

Kibbeh Nayyeh (Raw Kibbe)

- 1 lb. (500 grams) lean lamb meat, very fresh
- 2 large onions, quartered
- 4 oz. (100 grams) burgul (bulgur wheat)
- salt and pepper

Soak the burgul in water for 30 min. Squeeze out the liquid. Soften burgul with your hands. Chop the meat very fine. In a food processor, pulse the onions until they are liquidized. Add the meat paste, salt, and pepper. Puree the mixture until smooth then add the burgul. Spread the raw *kibbeh* on a flat serving dish. You can garnish the *kibbeh* with roasted pine nuts or parsley. Sprinkle some oil over the meat. Use Arabic bread as a scoop. Eat the meat together with sprigs of spring onions.

Note: Pregnant women and those with compromised immune systems should not consume raw meat.

Kibbeh with Cheese

- 2 lbs. (1 kg) lean lamb meat
- 1/2 lb. (250 grams) feta cheese

- 1 egg
- 1/2 cup (80 grams) of fine burgul (bulgur wheat)
- 2 medium onions
- 2 crushed cloves of garlic
- salt and pepper
- cinnamon
- hot chili pepper
- olive oil

Mix the meat with egg, burgul, finely cut onions, garlic, pepper, salt, and hot chili pepper to get a homogenous dough. Cut the feta cheese into small pieces. Take a small quantity of the dough, flatten it in your palm, place a piece of the cheese on the dough, and form a small ball with the cheese in the middle. Heat the oil in a pan and fry the meat balls quickly. As the meat and the cheese react differently to the frying, the meat balls can open and the cheese can come out. Therefore, make sure the oil is very hot, turn the balls around while frying, and remove quickly when ready.

As long as there was a problem in preserving meat, animals were kept alive until shortly before the cooking. That brought problems with keeping them, especially if a family lived in a flat in a city. In some regions there was a solution for this, like in the city of Sanaa in Yemen. There are, interestingly, many-storied traditional houses where one can see special round baskets hanging out of the windows. In these baskets, chicken can be kept alive for some days until slaughtering. In other cases, animals could be kept on the flat roofs of houses. But generally, the problem of keeping meat fresh was solved only with the introduction of refrigerators, and especially of deep freezers. Modern markets and butchers now have cooling houses where meat can be stored for a longer period. The consequence of this was that meat became a more interesting product and consumer good. The production increased and, especially in the rich oil-producing countries, the consumption of meat increased constantly.

There have been negative consequences for the health of the population. The need for refrigerators and deep freezers, of course, makes families dependent on the energy supply. If the security of this supply is in danger or is in constant risk, meat is a problematic food, even in a modern society. This was experienced by the inhabitants of Baghdad during the hot summer of 2003, when the electricity system failed because of the American military operation and the insecurity of the public life that followed. Many Baghdadi families had filled their deep freezers with meat and other kinds of food. When the electrical system failed, they could do nothing but throw the spoiled food out on the street, where is made an awful smell for weeks because the garbage-disposal service did not function.

In coastal regions, fish is a staple for both rich and poor families. At least in some parts of the Near and Middle East, such as Turkey, as well as in North Africa, fish, like bread, is considered to be a symbol of fertility. There is a Muslim saying that God had sent down to Jesus, the son of Mary, a table with five loaves of bread and two fish, and after having fed more the 5,000 persons, there were still 12 baskets of fish and bread left. Besides these religious explanations, there are more mundane reasons for the use of fish in regions where it is relatively easy to get. Compared with meat, fish has always been a cheaper kind of food. This, again, has to do with the fact that it has to be used as quickly as possible after the catch, especially in hot regions, so fishermen always have to sell it as soon as they come into the harbor. There is, of course, a tradition of drying fish, but people prefer fresh fish, and also did so in earlier times. In most cases, it is grilled and ready for eating more quickly than meat, so the cost of fuel was not important.

Generally, the ordinary meal of a middle-class family in towns or villages consists of a first and a main course and some sweets or fruit. In the Fertile Crescent region, there is the tradition of the *mezze*, which consists of starters with no limits of variety or quantity. It can be as simple as bread, yogurt, spearmint leaves, and olives, but the bread can come in different forms, and there may be the addition of raw vegetables like carrots or green peppers. On other occasions, the starters may be pickles, dips, cold vegetable dishes, stuffed vegetables, and cheese. Many of the first-course recipes take longer to prepare.

This is especially the case with chickpea or eggplant dips, which are very much loved all over the Near and Middle East and North Africa. Dried chickpeas have to be soaked in water overnight and cooked for some time afterward, whereas eggplants first have to be roasted and the skin peeled later. Even if chickpeas can be softened with a special high-pressure pot in less time, some preparation and organization are still required. So modern housewives prepare a greater quantity of this kind of food, so that they have enough for two or three days kept in the refrigerator. Store-bought dips in tins can also be bought, as can other starters such as stuffed grape leaves.

Even with an ordinary meal, the *mezze* always retains a flexible character. For instance, bread, yogurt, and spearmint leaves can be consumed separately. The diners can also feel free to mix them by dipping the bread into the yogurt and adding one or more spearmint leaves. Parsley can be used instead of spearmint. Some housewives serve, from time to time, all the leftovers out of their refrigerator in combination with round, flat Arabic bread as a first course. North African starters can be more complicated, and therefore the first course there is less flexible than that of the Middle East. Therefore, one can find more often light soups for the beginning of the meal. Simple soups consist of water, oil, garlic, peppermint leaves, tomatoes, *harisa* (a hot allspice), eggs, and bread. Another similar soup contains tomatoes, garlic, flour, oil, thyme, salt, and pepper. This type of soup can be thickened with chickpeas, beans, or noodles. Bouillon is also made from the bones and meat of sheep or veal.

Another kind of North African starter is the salad. The typical ones often consist of vegetable and fruit, which makes a quite-unusual combination. For example, tomatoes, peppers, cheese, olives, and apples are combined in a marinade of olive oil, vinegar, dried peppermint leaves, and salt. Another interesting combination is raw, grated, or rasped carrots with oranges, sugar, ground cinnamon, and salt. Strange but lovely is the combination of oranges with early or regular radish or even with cucumbers. Another combination is raw onions, small pieces of the flesh of citrons and, parsley. All these salads can be described as starters or first courses.

It is more difficult to define another type of North African dish: *brik*, or *briouat*. In Tunisia, *brik* is clearly a starter. It consists of a thin layer of dough filled with an egg. But the filling can vary—cooked vegetables, or even cooked meat. As this dish is fried in oil, it has to be considered a more heavy starter. The advantage of *briks* is that it is normally eaten lukewarm or nearly cold. That means that the housewife can prepare it in advance, and even bring it to the table before the family sits down. Still, the preparation is complicated and takes time, so since about the 1980s, this dish can be bought deep-frozen in many shops and is also exported to Europe, where working migrants from North Africa are the main consumers.

In between first course and the main part of the meal is a complicated Moroccan dish called *bstilla*. It is prepared in the following way: Six doves are cut into pieces and marinated for several hours with onions, garlic, saffron, ginger, parsley, pepper, salt, and olive oil. Then the meat is fried in oil or butter. One or more leaves of a thin dough, comparable to phyllo dough or the German *blätterteig*, are put on a cake tin. Onto this is put a mixture of ground almonds, powdered sugar, orange-blossom water, and cinnamon, which is covered again with a layer of dough. The next layer is the meat. Instead of doves, one can also use chicken. Some housewives add hard-boiled eggs to that. Then some powdered sugar is put over the meat. This again is covered with layers of dough. The construction is put into the oven until it is brown. Before serving, powdered sugar is sieved over the dish. Whether this recipe is served as a first or as main course depends on the quantity. As it is quite a sweet dish, it is questionable if one needs a sweet dessert after.

Main courses are usually meat or fish. As meat is expensive in the everyday kitchen, the meat course is normally a combination of some pieces of meat cooked in a combination of vegetables. The kind of vegetables depends on the season. Often the meat has been cooked or fried or grilled in advance and may be a leftover. The vegetable combination can include onions, carrots, radishes, pepperonis, generally tomatoes, more rarely potatoes, ladyfingers, eggplants, peppers, and whatever else is available. These vegetables are cooked in some water with olive oil or another fat, and the meat is added. Spices include salt and pepper and sometimes garlic, thyme, or sumac. The dish often has a greater quantity of liquid and a souplike consistency. Normally this is a very simple dish that is eaten with bread or rice, which is soaked with the liquid. Therefore it is eaten often with a spoon and/or with flat bread formed like a spoon.

In North Africa, the role of rice or bread is taken by couscous. The couscous is put in a special sieve over a broth of vegetables and meat and the steam will cook it. The vegetables can be carrots, radishes, onions, and tomatoes. Garlic is only used rarely, but in many recipes one finds chickpeas. The meat can be small pieces of lamb, veal, goat, or chicken, and sometimes one also finds minced meat instead of the whole piece. Of course, fish can also be used instead of meat. One can also prepare a sweet couscous, which is eaten for dessert. After the cooking, the couscous is served, and the vegetables and the meat with some liquid are served separately. Each person puts the couscous on his or her plate and soaks it with the broth, adding some of the vegetables and the meat. This method has the advantage that even with only a small quantity of meat, a complete and filling dish can be offered to the family. With this cooking technique, the taste of the dish is normally mild, so many love to add a hot sauce to the couscous with vegetables. This spicy sauce is prepared with *harisa*, a hot mixture of dried chilies, garlic, salt, coriander, cumin, and olive oil. This combination is prepared from time to time in great quantities but can also be store-bought. For use with couscous, *harisa* is mixed with tomato pulp and some broth. Every eater takes from this spice the quantity he prefers. In some recipes, raisins that have been soaked in water or broth before are added. All these additions, although unusual for Western eaters, make for an impressive and pleasant-tasting dish.

Berber woman making couscous, Matmata, Tunisia.
© Art Directors/TRIP Helene Rogers.

Another way to fix couscous is to put it directly into the broth with a great quantity of vegetables and meat. The couscous should absorb the broth, but the dish should not be too dry. This main course is so popular because the housewife can prepare is according to the season, amount of money on hand, and so on. There is one other North African main course, a more expensive meat course. But is has also some advantages. This dish in Morocco is called *tajine*. It takes its name from the pot in which it is prepared. A *tajine* consists of two pieces of pottery, which are often glazed on one side. The first part is a plate with a low rim. The second part is a high conic lid. There are simple and cheap ones as well as richly decorated, expensive ones on the market. One can buy them in at least nine different sizes. The *tajine* was traditionally used on an open fire, but today is put on a gas or electric flame or in an oven. Before using the *tajine* for the first time, one has to "cook it in." That means that one fills it with onions, carrots, garlic, water, and olive oil; covers it with its conic lid; and puts it into a hot stove for 30–40 minutes. After that, the vegetables are thrown away and the *tajine* is washed. With this preparation, the clayish smell is gone.

Cooking with a *tajine* is quite simple, and as most of the cooking is done on low heat, this technique has the advantage of reduced fuel usage. The plate is put on the fire, and butter or olive oil is added. The onions are softened, and the meat or fish is added and browned. Then it is covered with water, the heat is reduced, the conic lid it put on the plate, and the whole is simmered until the meat or fish is tender. With meat this can take up to two hours. It is sometimes necessary to add some water. If the meat is ready, it is taken out of the *tajine* and put in a warm place. Then various ingredients should be added. Almonds, dates, dried figs, dried plums, and many other items are options. After these have been heated and absorbed some of the liquid, the meat is put back onto the plate, and then the covered *tajine* is served. If it is a big one, it is put into the middle of the table, so that everyone can serve themselves, but there is also the custom of serving one small *tajine* for each person, especially if it is necessary to serve different types of dishes. *Tajine* is normally served with bread and not with couscous, rice, noodles, or potatoes.

Even in a single region, such as North Africa, different dishes bear the same name. In Tunisia, a *tajine* is also prepared in one pot, but traditionally in a quite different way. This technique is used, even today, when there is no electric stove. A big iron pot is placed in a great quantity of glowing charcoal. Then the pot is filled with the ingredients, and the lid is put upside down on the pot. More glowing charcoal is put onto the lid. Of course, this is a more complicated and time-consuming dish, because the heating of the coal and the cooking process take time, so it was generally prepared on special occasions. The ingredients of this Tunisian *tajine* consist in most cases of pieces of deboned lamb, water, fat or oil, and eggs. The eggs are curdled with small crumbs of bread. There are *tajines* with bread, noodles, onions, tomatoes and tomato pulp, beans, sweet or hot peppers, eggplants, cucumber, cheese, intestines, lamb sausages, minced meat balls, and much more. The spices are salt and pepper, often saffron, and hot *harisa* sauce.

In countries such as Iran or in the gulf region where rice predominates over bread or couscous, one can detect some parallels to the North African situation. Again, this has to do with the method and the costs of heating. Here also, traditionally, one tries to cook with as little fuel as possible. At the same time, every housewife tries to use all the leftovers in these recipes, or, with many wives working outside the house, they need to be efficient. So they prepare greater quantities of rice when they have time for that. The next day, meat is fried and vegetables are cooked. When these are ready, the rice is added and stirred so that the meat and the vegetables are combined with the rice equally. Now the mixture is soaked with one-half of a combination of yogurt, egg yolk, water, and salt. The rice is stirred again. Then the rest of the yogurt mixture and some butter are put on top of the rice. The pot is put into the stove on medium heat for about two hours. As one can imagine, there are many possible combinations of meat and vegetables. One can also use fish, and there are even some recipes where meat and fruit are combined. There are no special rules for the ingredients, and the knowledge, imagination, and creativity of the cook can always come up with new combinations. This type of recipe has gained in popularity with modern families because with the chaotic traffic situation in some of the Iranian cities, it is not certain when the members of the family will arrive home for the main meal of the day—if this rice pot is kept in the stove for 20 to 30 minutes more, it is OK.

Besides the dishes cooked in one pot, the modern cooks in the Near and Middle East and North Africa cook several dishes separately and serve them together in different bowls or plates. These may consist of meat, chicken, or fish as the main part of the meal; vegetables and bread; couscous; rice; or noodles. Potatoes are still not too accepted, although fried potatoes such as french fries are advancing in the culinary catalog. Today electric grills are fairly common in the modern kitchens, and lamb or chicken meat is often grilled. But, of course, everybody says that the charcoal grill is much better. Chicken is used more often than lamb or veal. Meat in general is now produced especially for human consumption, and the animals are therefore quite young when slaughtered, so the meat is tender after the grilling, if prepared the right way. Also, fish and other crustaceans are grilled. Normally, they are not marinated and only salted. For eating, spices and sauces or dips are offered separately, so that the diners can decide how they would like to have their part. For these dishes, of course, everyone has to be at the table at the same time.

Chicken is cut up and fried in butter or oil. The fried chicken pieces can be combined with many different ingredients, such as almonds and the various types of nuts, with pomegranate kernels, and with many spices. There are no rules for these combinations. Take, for example, a recipe with chicken and yogurt. The chicken is fried and almonds are added. Next, yogurt spiced with sumac is added to the meat. The sour taste of the yogurt with the sweetness of the almonds and the chicken gives an interesting contrast. Lamb, goat, or veal is cut into pieces and roasted with some vegetables like onions and carrots, with a later addition of almonds or nuts. Fish in coastal regions is, of course, very popular as a main course. Here one can find recipes where it is served separately from vegetables and other foods. A remarkable number of recipes have fish or crustaceans stuffed with vegetables, nuts, or bread crumbs. So sardines and mackerels are stuffed, as well as squids and mussels.

Even the housewife of a poorer family will try to find something to end the meal. The dessert may be quite simple and consist only of some fruit or the rest of a cake or some simple sweets. Children, of course, always ask for ice cream. Cheese as a last course is not common in the Near and Middle East and North Africa, even in families who follow a more European style of cooking. As the preparation of many of the sweets and desserts is quite complicated and time consuming, these are usually bought at special shops on the way home. These sweets consist of fat, honey, and nuts, and are caloric bombs. But some other desserts can be prepared at home quickly and easily. Most of these are types of puddings. One of the most famous is the *muhallabiyya*, a milk pudding. It is made from milk, corn flour or cornstarch, sugar, rose water, and cardamom. From the corn flour and some of the milk a paste is formed. The milk is boiled with sugar and cardamom. Then the paste is slowly stirred into the milk with a wooden spoon and simmered at a low heat until thickened. Then the rose water is stirred in and kept simmering for a few minutes. The *muhallabiyya* is then poured into a bowl or serving dish and kept cool for at least two

Lebanese patisserie selling typical Middle Eastern desserts, Amioun, Lebanon. © TRIP/H. Rogers.

hours. Before serving, it is sprinkled with almonds or pistachios and some drops of honey. Compared with other Near and Middle Eastern and North African desserts, the *muhallabiyya* is not extremely sweet. This dish can be prepared easily by every housewife or cook. It can also be bought ready-made. In the bazaar of Istanbul or Aleppo, one can still find a *muhallabci*, a specialist for the preparation of this dessert. But, of course, this is more expensive than home cooking.

Burtuqal Bi-L-Qirfa (Orange and Cinnamon Salad) (Dessert to Serve 10)

- 10 oranges
- 1/2 cup (100 grams) sugar
- 3/4 cup (100 ml) olive oil
- 2 tbsp. ground cinnamon
- some small mint leaves

Peel the oranges carefully and cut into thin slices, and arrange on a large plate in a fan shape. Add the sugar and sprinkle with the oil. Then dust the cinnamon over it and decorate with little mint leaves. Serve cold.

Technological development, especially in the kitchen, has not been unnoticed by the families of the Near and Middle East and North Africa. With everyday meals, many innovations are generally accepted. This development in a more general way started in the second half of the twentieth century. In all households with electricity or gas, refrigerators and deep freezers have made the life of the housewife easier, because the complicated and time-consuming task of conserving food is much more simple now. Also, cooking with gas or electric flames and stoves has made the cooking simpler, quicker, and less dangerous. Innovation with food started with canned products, the first of which was tomato pulp. Canned products such as ladyfingers, chickpeas, beans, and fruit, especially peaches, soon followed. Canned products were used now and then until the 1970s, but nobody confessed that he or she had been using them.

This attitude towards ready-made or partly prepared food changed with the introduction of deep-frozen food where one can buy it—mostly in the big cities and in some more Westernized parts of the region. The introduction of deep-frozen food went hand in hand with a tendency for a growing number of women to work outside the home to supplement the family income, so they have no time anymore for the complicated and time-consuming recipes they had learned from their mothers. This problem of time management could not be solved by the introduction of the modern kitchen equipment, so deep-frozen food came at the right moment. But, also, the trend of ready-made food brought home from a pizza or hamburger shop is growing. At home, this food is rewarmed. The problem is that some women feel guilty taking shortcuts, and there is a constant discussion among women on this topic.

NOTE

1. Andrea Rugh, *Family in Contemporary Egypt* (Syracuse: Syracuse University Press, 1984), 17.

5

Eating Out

STREET FOOD

Having a snack in the street or park or in the bus has always been an established habit in the Near and Middle East and North Africa for men and children only. Women will rarely be seen eating on the street; perhaps ice cream or some fruit is possible, but not more. The traditional snacks consumed are hot and cold ones. Cold ones include sandwiches; cakes and many types of sweets; and the special kinds of bread, which differ from country to country. One can get also salads and pickled vegetables. Nuts and olives are also offered. Hot snacks are, first of all, the famous *döner* dishes (see chapter 3). For the passersby, the *döner* meat is often put into a round, flat bread with additional tomatoes or a green lettuce leaf. In other dishes, the meat is put into bread and eaten. In Turkey, this is called *lahmajun*. It is a baked circle of dough thinly spread with a paste of ground lamb, green pepper, onion, parsley, and spices. It is served in all sorts of restaurants, but also in the streets. But there is also grilled or roasted chicken for takeout. Nowadays pizza and hamburgers are bought and eaten on the street. As described in chapter 4, many persons, especially in the big cities, are forced to buy some of their daily food from sellers on the streets or at bus or railway stations. Young men particularly like to treat their friends to a *döner* and a soft drink while discussing politics or sports events and speaking, of course, about girls on the street.

In some Near and Middle Eastern and North African countries, especially in the Fertile Crescent region, there is a common tradition of pic-

Carving doner meat, Istanbul, Turkey. © Art
Directors/TRIP Helene Rogers.

nicking. On days off for religious or public festivals, families and groups of
friends, soccer teams, and the like prepare various kinds of food and drink
and leave their quarters to visit parks or the countryside to eat and drink
together. Most of the dishes for a picnic are eaten cold, such as dips and
certain vegetables, meat (especially chicken), fruit, and sweets. Often the
picnickers have blankets or even a carpet that is spread on the ground. Others bring camping chairs and camping tables. Glasses, cups, and plates are
also part of the outdoor equipment. If it is possible, meat or fish is grilled.
There is also a custom to bury a whole sheep or even a camel in hot ashes.
Apart from eating and drinking, picnics are an opportunity to talk and
gossip, and there are always some musical instruments, especially drums, to
accompany folk songs and other popular songs. This custom of picnics has
been brought with migrant workers to western Europe. During summer in
the big parks of the cities, these immigrants have picnicked, much to the
astonishment of the Europeans, who now follow this practice.

The separation of the sexes is still a topic in modern Near and Middle Eastern and North African societies. Depending on the degree of modernization of the individual family, the possibility of social exchange between men and women is greater today than it was 50 years ago, but it is still quite unusual to invite persons who are not related into the house for a meal with the family. Exceptions are made for foreigners, who stay only for a short time in the country. Of course, visits are possible, but these are visits among the same sex: women visit women, and men visit men. During these visits only drinks, soft drinks, or coffee or tea (and in some cases alcoholic drinks) and little snacks are offered. Visits by relatives are something else. These are quite regular and have a formal as well as an informal character. Relatives who drop in unexpectedly during a meal will be asked to join the table. On special occasions like big religious festivals or individual feasts of the family, formal invitations are made for big receptions and lavish meals.

The gender restrictions between unrelated persons hinder social contacts, as it is impossible to invite couples or individuals to the house. Therefore, other forms of social intermingling have become very successful in Near and Middle Eastern and North African societies. One of them is eating out. This does not mean that the gender restrictions are overcome, but at least it is possible for persons of the same sex to invite each other to coffeehouses, restaurants, or bars.

Coffeehouses in the Near and Middle East and North Africa are places with a restricted number of items offered to the customers. In some cases they have only simple furniture. These can consist of only some cheap chairs made of plastic or a traditional material like wood or reed. Tables are of the same kind. Some of these places are only operated during seasons without rain, because they are in open air and the keeper of this establishment only has a hut where he stores soft drinks and the equipment that is needed for the preparation of coffee or tea. Food is not offered except some sweets, which are also asked for by the children of the neighborhood. The owner of the coffeehouse also sells cigarettes and sometimes has water pipes for his guests. Normally there is also a radio playing or the blaring sounds of music from an audio tape. The prices at these places are very low, and the owner will not be angry if his guests stay with one bottle of a soft drink or one glass of tea for hours and hours.

More esteemed coffeehouses are situated in buildings in the center of the big cities. Their furniture is more comfortable. An air conditioner is running (often more chilling than cooling), or one or more fans are turning the air on the ceiling. Besides nonalcoholic drinks, various cakes are on the menu card. Some of theses places are famous for their special sweets. In many cases a television set is running, and the customers pay attention only when sports events such as soccer or boxing are on. The prices here are higher, but there are also waiters. Some of these places are quite famous, because artists, writers, and other intellectuals meet there regularly and try to solve the problems of their society or those of the world. These more traditional places are frequented only by men. Respectable women would never enter places like that.

The same holds true, of course, for bars and establishments where alcohol is served. Concerning these places, there has been a remarkable change during the last 50 years. Up to the end of the 1960s, in side streets of the modern parts of Near and Middle Eastern and North African cities, there were places where one could get alcoholic drinks, mostly beer. No signs or advertisements outside hinted at the character of establishment. Outside as well as inside there was little light. These simple establishments often had only a bar and some bistro tables, but no chairs. Here one could get local beer with some snacks such as salted almonds, pistachios, or potato chips. The price for the beer was relatively high. Often the beer was brought without a glass, so that one had to drink directly from the bottle. Normally there was no music. Everything was done to keep the profile of these places as low as possible. Women never entered these places. The owner and his helpers who acted as security guards saw to it that nobody drank too much, and they stopped every quarrel between customers right at the beginning. Unlike better coffeehouses and cafés, beggars could enter these places and ask the sinners for some money, which was normally given. The owners were supervised closely by the police, and it may be that there was always some relation to organized crime. These places could be found in countries like Egypt, Syria, or Iraq and Iran before the Islamic Revolution. In strict Islamic countries like Saudi Arabia and some of the Gulf Emirates, these establishments never existed. Since the middle of the 1970s, these places have disappeared completely with the re-Islamization of the Near and Middle Eastern and North African societies.

One other possibility of eating out in the Near and Middle East and North Africa is at clubs. Particularly in that part that was under British colonial rule, clubs were installed according to various social aspects. One was that of status. From the early 1930s, important families became members of these clubs, which have large premises with gardens, swimming pools, tennis lawns, restaurants, bars, libraries, and so on. The clubs offer cinema programs, lectures, bingo, dancing, and more. Often club fees are quite high, and there were and still are strict rules regarding who could enter, how many guests could be brought, and so on. Other clubs are organized according to profession. There are clubs of teachers, doctors, lawyers, and (very important) officers. Membership is less expensive, and the amenities are, in many cases, less high-end. But these clubs are also important places for social interaction.

In all these clubs, it is possible to invite acquaintances, business partners, friends, or relatives for lunch, dinner, or just a snack. As some of these clubs have a contract with a nearby restaurant or hotel, even more attractive dishes can be offered. For many members, these clubs are their second home where they spend most of their free time, meet friends, and invite new acquaintances. Here they feel free from some of the social rules that exist outside the club. What happens to the social interaction if these clubs do not function anymore could be observed in Iraq in the 1990s. Because of the breakdown of the economic structure from the UN embargo, most of the Iraqi middle class had no money to continue with membership in these clubs and had to stay home all the time, so the social interaction of this class of Iraqi society came to a stop. This is one of the reasons why the Iraqi middle class dissolved and has to be reconstructed again now.

In big cities of the region, there are also clubs organized in cooperation with international hotel chains. The members of these clubs can use the hotel amenities such as swimming pools, tennis courts, bars, and restaurants. The cultural and social programs of these clubs are, compared with the other types of clubs, often reduced. There is no cinema and no lectures and other cultural events. Therefore the membership fees are often lower, but still high enough that not everybody has the means to enter the club. The hotel clubs are attractive especially for those Middle Easterners who are interested in having contact with the international clientele of these hotels for various reasons, such as improving their capacity in a foreign language, getting information about foreign societies and political developments, and making social contacts.

These clubs tend to serve crossover cuisine. Generally one can find the culinary structure of starters, main courses, and sweets, like on any traditional table, but there are variations in the quantities. Whereas in the traditional meal the starters often have the greatest quantity and are considered very important, in the club kitchen the main course is the more important dish. The starters, here, are only small in number and quantity. Of course, there are always some recipes coming from the local or regional tradition, but there are also hors d'oeuvres from international cuisine. The main courses consist of grilled meat or fish, and often in greater quantities. Sweets are often also from international cookbooks. The quality of the food in these clubs varies. There is what one might call a tradition of complaining about the food in the club. Female members are especially strong critics, and often one can hear comments like that one can only eat meat or fish—anything else one should eat at home.

In many clubs it was also common to serve alcoholic drinks. Most of it was beer and Scottish whiskey in Egypt and parts of the Fertile Crescent that had been under British colonial influence. These were the typical alcoholic drinks for the males, while women took to gin and tonic. Wine was uncommon. While the local beer, often produced by German brewers or coming from Belgium, was acceptable, local wines were hard to get used to. In regions with French influence it was local or imported wine and cognac or other French spirits that were offered. Local strong liquors like *raki* or *arrak*, a drink flavored with aniseed, or *boukha*, a strong drink made of figs, were only rarely drunk in these clubs. After the re-Islamization of the Near and Middle Eastern and North African societies, alcoholic drinks were offered less frequently in these clubs. Especially during important religious times of the year like Ramadan, the Muslim month of fasting, even more liberal clubs offer no alcohol.

Restaurants offering food and nonalcoholic drinks are a more recent phenomenon in the Near and Middle East and North Africa. Prepared food had been offered in the bazaar in the Middle Ages, but these dishes were taken home and eaten there. Places where one could consume a meal with wine existed, but alcohol was the main reason to visit.[1] Generally, these places had a poor reputation, were constantly supervised by the authorities, and had to pay special taxes. Only in places where travelers such as traders or pilgrims spent the night was some food offered. As the issue of ritual cleanness was always important, the believers of the different confessions and religions tried to avoid contact with persons of other religions while eating. Traveling members of the religious minorities often went to their religious institutions, such as convents or synagogues, where they could either spend the night or were informed about hostels. Travelers without friends or family were hosted by other believers of their faith. Spending a night under the same roof of a private home was and still is nearly impossible for members of different religions in the Near and Middle East and North Africa. Eating together is easier nowadays, but this is a recent development. Although the prophet Muhammad had allowed his followers to eat what Jews or Christians had offered them, in some parts of the Near and Middle East and North Africa it was impossible for non-Muslims to eat in a restaurant managed by Muslims. Up to the 1920s, in areas of Shiite inhabitants, non-Shiite customers in restaurants run by Shiite owners were either not served, or their plates and bowls were broken after they had been used. Like in hostels where blankets were washed separately when non-Shiites had slept in them, even in the 1950s, dishes used by non-Shiites were cleaned in special tubs.

Today, in nearly all small and big cities of the Near and Middle East and North Africa, different types of restaurants can be found. In little towns and in the traditional quarters of big cities, their number is always few and they have a limited menu. Only a written sign outside states that there is a restaurant and, perhaps, gives the name of the owner. In other cases, the restaurant may have a name. The name is chosen by the owner, perhaps to attract a certain kind of customer. For instance, he may call his place Republican Restaurant, or a religious name such as Restaurant of the Cross, from which it becomes clear that the owner is a Christian who wants to attract his fellow believers. There may also be national indicators, such as when a restaurant is called Palestine. Mostly the names of these traditional restaurants are less telling. They may be called Star of the South, or just Star, and there are many other name of celestial bodies. There are geographical names, like Nile Restaurant or Restaurant of the Desert. Perhaps such a sign is lit at night, but in most cases one can see the sign only during daytime. In most cases the names of the restaurant are nondescriptive.

Often these restaurants have only a few tables, without tablecloths, and wooden or plastic chairs without cushions. The plates and bowls used in these restaurants are made of cheap porcelain that does not break easily. If the customers do not eat by hand, simple knives, forks, or spoons are available. On the wall of such restaurants might be a photograph of the head of state or another important political person or a sports star. A TV set, radio, or tape player may blare, but nobody pays much attention. Often the restaurants are dark because of the small windows and little electric light. Sometimes there is an air conditioner, but more often only a fan at the ceiling. Not all the restaurants of this type have toilets, but often one can wash one's hands.

Typically these traditional restaurants have two sections. The bigger one is for male customers only. Another part is called the "family section." Here men and women can eat together, often accompanied by several children. Women on their own will not enter such a place. Customers are normally males on their own, young employees without family, students living too far from their family, and other men living alone who have no time to cook for themselves or do not know how. They have a small but regular income and can afford a simple meal every day.

These restaurants open at noon. Some of them will have a break in the afternoon and open again at about 7 P.M. and will be closed after 10. The restaurant staff is all male, but one can imagine that some of the food that is offered has been prepared by a woman in the owner's family the day or the night before. Some of these restaurants have been owned by one family for several generations. The knowledge of how to run such a place is passed down from fathers to sons. In this type of restaurant, there is no written menu. The owner, who is often the waiter and cook at the same time, will bring some water and glasses and then announce in a loud voice what he has to offer. He may suggest some dishes or ask the customer whether he wants something special. He will not mention the price while offering his dishes. If there is a cook in a separate kitchen, the waiter will shout through the restaurant what should be prepared, so all customers know what everybody is eating that day. Regular customers know the prices. What the waiter is offering can be served within minutes because it is already prepared. The dishes are simple—for example, some cooked lamb with onions, ladyfingers, tomatoes, salt, and pepper. This is served with bread or rice. Stuffed vegetables are also common. Generally the dishes can be cooked, or at least kept warm for many hours until everything is sold. The customers normally eat quickly and even hastily. If the customer wants something special, it can take some time until it is served, because it has to be prepared from scratch, and perhaps some of the ingredients have to be bought at the market. It is also possible to bring some kind of food to be prepared by the cook as the customer likes it. This could be, for instance, a special fish or fowl that is not generally on the menu.

Besides cooled water, soft drinks are offered, but no alcoholic drinks. After eating, some of the customers have coffee or tea. In some of the traditional restaurants, men prepare these drinks as a business. They bring the coffee or tea, which they have prepared in a corner of the restaurant, and collect the money. In some cases, they pay the owner a small sum every day; in other cases it is a kind of charity, especially if the vendor of these drinks is handicapped.

If there are groups of young men eating together in these restaurants, they normally do not treat each other, because this would be too expensive for some of them, and it would not be acceptable because the poorer ones could not act reciprocally. But with the hot drink after the meal it is different, and one of the group might treat the others to a glass of tea or cup of coffee. Especially in the evening, several rounds of these glasses are ordered and paid for by different friends.

Mansaf (Arabic, for 10 or More Persons)

- 10 lbs. (about 5 kg) leg of lamb, jointed
- 10 chopped large onions
- 6 crushed cloves of garlic
- 5 tbsp. lemon juice
- 2 cups yogurt
- 2 large Arabic breads
- 1/2 cup (250 grams) rice
- 1/4 cup (125 grams) mixed almonds and pine nuts
- oil
- water

Let the yogurt drain overnight in a linen towel. Heat the oil in a big pot or pan, sauté the onions and garlic, and then add the meat and sauté until slightly brown. Cover with water and let simmer until tender. Remove the scum that rises. Now prepare the rice with nuts as usual. Take the lamb out of the stock, cut into pieces, and keep the meat warm. Reduce the stock and add the dried yogurt. Stir in the lemon juice. To serve the *mansaf,* open the Arabic bread and place it on a tray. Place the rice with nuts on the bread in large quantities; on the rice, place the pieces of meat. The stock is served separately.

Since the mid-1960s, special chicken restaurants appeared in central places in the big Near and Middle Eastern and North African cities. This was a consequence of the beginning of the industrial production of chicken there, which again was possible because of the development of deep freezing. In the Fertile Crescent, chicken production on a larger scale was started first in Lebanon. When this production broke down because of the civil war in the 1970s, deep-frozen chicken was imported from Europe. Consequently, especially on the Arab peninsula, a discussion arose about whether it was allowed for Muslims to consume meat that was produced by Christians. The same issue came up in Morocco. Muslim religious authorities ruled that Muslims could eat this meat in general, but some French and Danish companies saw to it that the Muslim slaughtering regulations were observed, and Muslim authorities proved this by certificates that were attached to every deep-frozen chicken. Today much of the chicken is produced in the Near and Middle East and North Africa by local companies. These chicken restaurants were an immediate success for several reasons. First, chicken had been held in high esteem for a long time. Traditional doctors saw it as a healthful and nourishing food. However, chicken in the pre-deep-freezer days was a rare and costly food on the normal table, so there was a run on chicken when it became available so easily.

The decor of the chicken restaurants is the same as in traditional restaurants: cheap and simple. Therefore, the ordinary people could feel comfortable. Many of them do not have a family section. That means that for some women it is difficult to enter. But generally, chicken restaurants are experienced as an aspect of modernity and Westernization.

Chicken restaurants offer grilled chicken only. The chickens are brought to the restaurants ready for the grilling; perhaps only the seasoning has to be done in the restaurant. The grilling machines first came from Europe, and today also come from Asia. The chicken is speared on long spits, with five or more on one of them. The grilling machine may contain three to five spits that rotate. Often there is no bread or rice, no soup, no vegetables, and no sweets. Sometimes it is even hard to get something to drink apart from cool water. The normal quantity of ordering is half a chicken. The price for this quantity is advertised outside the restaurant, and there is some competition between different chicken restaurants in this regard. The chicken is served very quickly, often without any questions. It is clear from the beginning that everybody entering such a place wants half a chicken. This is often served on a cardboard plate with a paper napkin. As one eats it by hand, no utensils are needed. The fingers are cleaned with the paper napkin, and in some establishments of this kind it might be possible to wash one's hands, but normally there is no toilet.

The chicken restaurants are open without interruption from about 11 A.M. until midnight. Most of these restaurants have a takeout section as well. Here one can buy whole or half chickens. There are special bags for transport to keep the food warm for some time. The owners of these chicken restaurants see to it that they have sold all the chicken they have grilled in one day, because chicken grilled on the day before is not accepted by the customers. Therefore the owners give away the last chicken of the day at a lower price, or they reduce the number of chickens for grilling in the later evening. At the beginning, chicken restaurants were seen as strong competitors on the market by the owners of traditional restaurants, but soon it became clear that the concentration on chicken was no competition, because the customers of traditional restaurants would not eat only chicken every day. For them, going to a chicken restaurant was and is still an exception to the daily food routine. It is a good option for families, because children are usually fond of chicken. For many of them, this is the first and often the only restaurant that they ever visit. The simple way of eating is part of the attraction of these places for children, but for adults, too.

Cerkez Tavugu (Shredded Chicken with Walnut and Coriander) (Turkish)

- 1 whole medium-sized chicken
- 3 slices dry white bread without crusts
- 1/2 cup (150 ml) milk
- 1 1/2 cups (200 grams) shelled walnuts
- 6 cloves of crushed garlic
- small bunch of fresh coriander leaves
- small bunch of fresh parsley
- salt and pepper
- 1 onion
- 4 cloves
- salt and pepper
- cinnamon
- olive oil
- water

Remove the excess fat from the chicken and put it into a large pan with the onion, cloves, pepper, salt, and cinnamon. Add water to cover it all. Bring the water to boil, cover the pan, and lower the heat, then let simmer for about 1 hour. When the chicken is tender, take it out of the stock and let it cool down until you can touch it. Remove the flesh from the bones. Discard the skin. Cut the meat into small strips and place into a large bowl. Reduce the stock by boiling for 30 min. Check the seasoning and strain the liquid. Soak the bread in milk, grind the walnuts, add the garlic to prepare a paste, and work it into the soaked bread. Add this mixture to the strips of chicken and bind together with spoonfuls of the warm seasoned liquid. Work all the liquid into the mixture until you have a light and creamy consistency. Add the roughly chopped coriander and parsley leaves. If not served immediately, add some olive oil to prevent the mixture from drying.

Modern Western-style restaurants were established in greater numbers in the Near and Middle East and North Africa in the 1950s and 1960s. First they could be found in the capitals and big cities. The founders were locals who had some experience with this type of restaurant because of trips to Europe or the Western world. In North Africa, but also in Lebanon and Syria, French nationals took the risk of establishing restaurants. In other Near and Middle Eastern and North African countries, religious minorities founded the first modern restaurants, sometimes with the money of silent Muslim shareholders. In many cases the staff was also from the Christian minorities and, especially in the gulf area, of Indian origin. The number of waiters and cooks coming from the majority population increased in many countries. There are only few exceptions. These are the rich oil countries where it is impossible for a local to work in the service domain. People working in these modern restaurants are normally male. Modern restaurants are situated in the central areas of big cities and in residential areas with well-to-do or foreign inhabitants, but they can also be found in smaller cities where tourists visit. In most cases, these restaurants have modern Western names, often with French terms. They may be called Tour d'Argent or Rotisseur, have elaborate electric signs, and advertise in the European-language papers of the region. Recently there has been a trend to use local names written in Latin characters, such as Al-Furat (Euphrates), Nil, or Umm Kulthum (the name of a famous Egyptian singer).

The furniture of modern restaurants is pretty typical of that in places of this kind in Western countries. Normally there are big windows and lamps in the evening, for atmosphere. Generally these places are air-conditioned. Often the temperature inside is so cold that customers coming in from the heat may catch a cold. Experienced travelers always carry a sweater. As for the decor, in Western-style restaurants it is typical to see one or even more pictures of the head of state at a strategic point. And there may be copies of well-known modern Western works of art at the walls. There may be flowers on the tables, and in some places a fountain. Chairs and tables are of high quality. Perhaps international music can be heard in the background. Tablecloths are linen. Sometimes one can observe waiters who put the cloth on the table as exactly as they had made their bed during their military service.

The staff normally has good standards. Many of the Near and Middle Eastern and North African countries have special schools for the personnel of hotels and restaurants that give good, internationally accepted training. In most countries the staff of the modern restaurants comes from the region. In the gulf countries, most service staff are expatriates either from other Arab countries or from South and Southeast Asia. Cooks and waiters have typical uniforms.

Besides Western-style restaurants, some modern ones have a Near and Middle Eastern or North African style and decor. These are also situated

Eating out, Zahleh, Lebanon. © Art Directors/TRIP Helene Rogers.

in central areas of cities and well-to-do quarters. They differ in style from the Western type. Tables are low, and one sits on cushions or low stools. The design of this furniture imitates traditional forms and is often of high artistic quality. Of course, here also one finds the unavoidable picture of the head of state together, perhaps, with the national flag. In many of these modern restaurants there is regional or Western music from tapes or CDs. The walls are decorated with calligraphies and copies from Near and Middle Eastern miniatures. Certainly there is a fountain or water running through the place. These restaurants are air-conditioned, too. While the cooks here also have their white working clothes, the waiters often wear regional clothes such as baggy trousers, embroidered shirts and jackets, and a fez or other similar hat.

Apart from the decor and the dress of the waiters, there is no difference in organization between the Western- and regional-style restaurants. Both have menus and will offer a wider selection of dishes and drinks. On the menu there are sections for starters, main courses of fish and meat, and fruit and sweets. Sometimes there may also be additional sections for soups and salads or cheese. Some modern restaurants offer complete menus of three to five or more courses. The prices will be listed, at least for male customers. For women accompanied by a man, there may even be a ladies' menu card without the prices. The prices are quite high and cannot be paid by ordinary customers, so they consist of upper-class people and foreigners.

What distinguishes the modern Western-style from the modern regional restaurants is, of course, the type of food that is offered. In the Western restaurants in the Near and Middle East and North Africa, one can have plates of European cuisine with a strong French influence. This is not only limited to the countries that had been under French colonial influence. Until the 1960s, French cuisine was seen as the peak of culinary refinement in the Near and Middle East and North Africa. Of course, only very few of these restaurants could reach the quality of their French prototypes. The number of starters was normally reduced and had dishes like avocado cream, some soups, or crustaceans. These were often canned. Main courses were often steak and potatoes, perhaps accompanied by a green salad. For the dessert one had fruit or a crème bavaroise or brûlée. For Near and Middle Easterners and North Africans, eating in this type of restaurant was an exotic experience that had nothing to do with the quality of the food, which could only be judged by a small number of customers. Nevertheless, many locals went to these restaurants on special occasions or tried to get an invitation there. In the meantime, the quality of the menu has improved. One of the reasons is that the ingredients used are imported by air from the producing regions, and some of the chefs and the other kitchen staff are from Europe. There are even special events when a famous European chef comes for one or more weeks to cook in a certain restaurant. For such a visit there will be special advertisements.

Since the mid-1980s, a change in these modern Western restaurants can be observed. From then on, the various European national cuisines were differentiated. Restaurants with a typical French program were established, where first-class cooks copied recipes of famous chefs such as Paul Bocuse or Paul Haeberlin. Even more successful were Italian restaurants. Like in many other countries, these restaurants started offering a variety of pizzas. In the meantime, the multifaceted Italian cuisine has taken over from the more simple pizza bakers. There are also a number of Spanish or Iberian restaurants. Other Western restaurants constantly shift style: one month Italian, the next French, Russian, or Scandinavian. Because of the importance of pork in German restaurants, these types are rare. This makes it clear that the way of cooking European national specialties in restaurants in the Near and Middle East and North Africa has to take into account the food taboos of Islam or Judaism. This means that recipes with alcohol such as wine or cognac, even if it is burned off, must be changed or cannot be offered. Recipes with pork or any other pork product must also be avoided. Dishes with gelatin cannot be made, for example.

The decor of these ethnic restaurants is also ethnic—so we find restaurants with Italian flags and pictures of Naples and Vesuvius or a picture of famous places in Rome. German restaurants look like a Bavarian or Tyrolian *gasthaus*. There is also, accordingly, German, Italian, or Spanish music on tape, changing with regional music. If the restaurant is shifting its European program regularly, there will be also a change of the decoration or the music. But all restaurants have the picture of the head of state, in these places perhaps from a state visit to that country, together with leading politician of that country.

Besides the Western-type restaurants, especially in big cities, today one can also find many restaurants with Indian, Chinese, or Japanese cuisine. Only a small number of Arab or Iranian clients frequent these establishments. One reason for their reluctance is that the prices are quite high, whereas the religious prohibitions do not play a role.

European or Eastern-style restaurants, for many Near and Middle Easterners and North Africans, have a touch of exotic flavor. That is why people who only visit expensive modern restaurants on special occasions normally prefer modern regional-style restaurants. Although many things are different from the simple traditional restaurants they visit, at least the food for them has some familiar aspects. Surely they will find the prices absurd and react with an embarrassed laughter. If the Near and Middle Eastern and North African customers of these restaurants are more experienced, they will take a glance at the menu and not order special starters, but instead a complete range of small snacks, the famous *mezze*. Sometimes only the *mezze* is ordered. That is a wise decision, because the number of small bowls and plates can be so numerous that one is completely full after having eaten all that is brought to the table. In that case, no main course is ordered, and perhaps only some dessert. In more liberal countries, the *mezze* in this type of restaurants will be accompanied with the local strong liquor, called *raki* in Turkey or *arrak* in Syria, Iraq, and Lebanon. It is a white brand from raisins, flavored with aniseed. With the *mezze* this drink is served always in a bottle, but very cool. To avoid the bottle warming, it is served with the glasses on crushed ice or ice cubes. Some customers put the glass back on the ice for cooling when they have emptied it. The liquor can be mixed with water. Then it will turn to a kind of white color. That is why it is called *halib al-asad* (milk of the lion). Those who are not accustomed to this drink underestimate its strength, because it is served so cool. There is a tradition that is passed from generation to generation of drinkers that *arrak* or *raki* does not cause a hangover if one avoids drinking water the next morning. But this is one of the many stories reported on the everyday life of the Near and Middle East and North Africa that should not be trusted too much.

Modern regional-style restaurants also offer a great variety of other first courses and several main courses. The menu has a variety of starters besides the *mezze*. One can have soups, salads, small portions of meat or fish, or dishes with eggs or pickled vegetables. If they are not part of the *mezze* they will come in greater quantities. In modern regional restaurants it is uncommon to have a starter, a fish course and, a meat course. The main dish is either fish or meat. For a normal Western eater, it is nearly impossible to find room for dessert. Consequently, the service staff does not press the customers to order desserts. More often one has the opposite impression. This is, of course, a pity, because the restaurants offer a variety of sweets, which are very complicated and time consuming to prepare at home. Only 20 years ago, the desserts were said to be very sweet because of their high portions of sugar and honey. Modern restaurants offer dishes for the sweet tooth that are not oversweet anymore. There is also a tendency nowadays to offer more light desserts or smaller portions. Fruit as a last course is always a possibility. When coffee is served, the meal is finished immediately and everybody leaves the table. That means that one does not sit for another half an hour just talking or relaxing. Alcoholic digestives are not common, even in restaurants where alcohol is served. In North Africa they have a hot black tea with fresh green mint that has, in fact, a digestive effect.

The service of modern regional restaurants can be somehow ritualistic. The same goes for Western-style restaurants in the Near and Middle East and North Africa. As the number of waiters does not play into the costs, there will be a headwaiter who takes the order, writes it down, and puts a copy of the order on the table. Often the headwaiter will reappear only for the bill. During the meal, now and again, waiters come and have a look at the copy. It is not possible to find a reason for that, because one or the other will never bring a dish to the table. Now and then in chic restaurants, the tablecloth is changed after every course of the menu. This is done in such a way that first the fresh tablecloth is spread over the used one, then the used one is taken away with a technique of rolling the used cloth together under the new one—an astonishing sight. In many modern restaurants, a young waiter comes with water, a bowl, and a towel to let the customers wash their hands. Of course, this is only an symbolic act, which is repeated after the meal. More effective is the custom of offering the clients after the meal sprinkles of orange-blossom essence from a special silver flacon with a long neck. Drops are put on the hands, and one also brings them to the face. This has, indeed, a freshening effect. Some of the modern regional restaurants of the higher quality later in the evening have live music, sometimes with famous, but always quite good and professional, musicians, and there may be also female singers and dancers.

International chain hotels often have modern Western-style and regional-style restaurants that are operated in the same way. As they are frequented by a larger portion of foreigners, tourists, and businesspeople, the regional-style ones are accustomed to Western ways of cooking and spicing. That means that in some of them there is a type of crossover kitchen that is described as Near and Middle Eastern and North African but that has a certain distance from that cuisine. Most of these hotels also have coffee shops where light meals are served all day. There is often a mixture of dishes of Western and regional origin offered. As the service is normally very quick, the coffee shops are frequented not only by the residents of the hotel, but also by many local and foreign passersby who have a quick lunch and meet with people in a lively atmosphere. As the prices are quite high, it is also only a certain clientele one can find in this place.

Some words should be said about the international fast-food chains one can find all over the Near and Middle East and North Africa, such as McDonald's, Burger King, and Kentucky Fried Chicken. They found their way to the Near and Middle East and North Africa in the late 1970s. Some of them are seen as typical representatives of U.S. culture, so the existence of these establishments is also a sign for the official political acceptance of the United States in general. If the general attitude of a political regime in the Near and Middle East and North Africa toward the United States changes, all branches of such a chain might be closed. Chain restaurants can also be the first targets of political popular unrest against the pro-Western politics of a government.

Fast-food chains try not to change their menu, no matter where a branch is opened. In the Near and Middle East and North Africa, of course, they have to consider the food taboos. This means that in Muslim countries there are no pork dishes. In Israel, there are also kosher McDonald's restaurants. Some of the chains, from time to time, have special offers, so there is room to conform to local customs. For example, the McDonald's branches in Cairo offer falafel during the holy month of Ramadan. Falafel is an Egyptian fast food that can be found in other parts of the Near and Middle East and North Africa. It has been noted that walking hungrily along the street in Arab countries, you turn the corner to almost certainly find a street-side stall with tasty, dark brown, crispy falafel. Your attention is immediately drawn to hand manipulating at lightning speed a shiny brass tool that identically shapes each mound of puréed beans. The mixture is spooned into the top of the tool, smoothed over, and then pushed out to deep-fry in a big black wok called a hala or saj. Buy some to appease the appetite, as the snack is only a few pence for a full bag. Before carrying them far you will be tempted to sneak a taste of these irresistibly warm and crumbly croquettes. The more patient (and less hungry) may wait for a rolled sandwich of Arabic bread, stuffed with broken falafel, tahina, mint parsley, lettuce, and sometimes tomatoes.[2]

Although it is fast food, and the other products are also considered to be fast food, a visit to McDonald's or Burger King for most Near and Middle Easterners and North Africans does not have the character of a fast-food meal. For them, these establishments are exotic places, for several reasons. First, the prices are high compared with the traditional fast-food places, so the customers of Casablanca, Cairo, or Istanbul who have to calculate with their meager income will go there only on special occasions. As in many other parts of the world, the clientele is normally young, but middle-aged persons also go there. The second reason for the exoticism is the Western atmosphere of the restaurant. It does not matter if these places are operated by local owners on a franchise basis or directly by the international or national companies, with the furniture, the menu, and the staff uniform all over the world.[3] One more reason is the food itself. After all, a hamburger is still a strange food for people in the Near and Middle East and North Africa. Eating with one's hand is not unusual, but the combination of bread, meat, vegetables such as onions and tomatoes, and cheese is something new. The big portion of meat is also important. As mentioned, meat plays a secondary role in the Near and Middle Eastern and North African diet.

Someone not acquainted with the United States or a McDonald's restaurant may think the American way of life strange. From the beginning, the Near and Middle Easterners and North Africans' reaction to these establishments was different from that of western Europeans. The first McDonald's restaurant opened near the Spanish Stairs in Rome and led to protests by artists and intellectuals and to the successful founding of a group of restaurants and chefs who advocate slow food. In the Near and Middle East and North Africa, the chains were welcomed by the younger generation as a sign of modernization, although there were some pessimists who feared for the culinary heritage.[4] This fear was not well founded. There are some reasons why the international chains could not outdo the traditional fast-food places in the region. The first is an economic one. Traditional fast food is still much cheaper than the dishes offered by the chains. People are much more used to it. They know what they get for their money. As they do not visit chain restaurants regularly, they are still unsure about the food they get there and the ratio between the price and what they get. The second is the food itself. Many people pride themselves on their culinary traditions and of their competence in cooking and especially tasting. They find the small and always identical menu of chain restaurants to be simply boring.

The relative success of chain restaurants also has something to do with the locations where they have been established since the 1990s. Shopping malls are a very new experience in the Near and Middle East and North Africa. People go there on weekends to window-shop or just spend the time in air-conditioned areas during the hot period of the year. Many shopping malls have these chain restaurants. They have to be seen in this context. The shopping malls differ very much from traditional shopping places (although mall owners compare them with the traditional bazaar areas of the old cities), as do the chain restaurants. So it is strange, and for many a little bit bizarre and novel, to go there.

In the last several years, fast-food chains have been started by Near and Middle Eastern and North African businessmen. These restaurants are working according to the same principles as the Western chains. They differ only in the menu offered. It is too early to discern whether these will succeed.

NOTES

1. Peter Heine, *Weinstudien: Untersuchungen zur Anbau, Produktion und Konsum des Weins im arabisch-islamischen Mittelalter* (Wiesbaden: Harrassowitz, 1982).

2. Miriam Al Hashimi, *Traditional Arabic Cooking* (Reading, UK: Garnet Publishing, 1993), 14–15.

3. For the history and business ideology of one of those international chains, see John F. Love, *McDonald's: Behind the Arches* (New York: Bantam Books, 1995).

4. Holly Chase, "The Meyhane or McDonald's? Changes in Eating Habits and the Evolution of Fast Food in Istanbul," in *Culinary Cultures of the Middle East*, ed. Sami Zubaida and Richard Tapper (London: Tauris, 1994), 73–85.

6

Special Occasions

Ordinary life is structured by working days and days off. In the countries of the Near and Middle East and North Africa, days off can be every Friday for Muslims, every Saturday for Jews, and every Sunday for Christians. In cities where all three religions were or still are present, this impacts the way of life. In modern Damascus, a remarkable number of shops in the bazaar area and in the modern city are closed on Sundays because the owners are Christians. Fifty years ago, the same could be said about Saturdays in Tehran and other Iranian cities, because of the important role Jews were playing in the economic life. Friday now is a quiet day because of the Muslim majority in the Near and Middle East and North Africa, with the exception of Israel. Other interruptions of the dull day-to-day routine are the great religious festivals that are repeated once a year, like the Muslim Feast of Sacrifice (*id al-adha*) and the feast at the end of the holy month of Ramadan (*id al-fitr*), which is a special month-long feast of its own. Other regular Muslim holidays commemorate of the birthday of the prophet Muhammad (*mawlid al-nabi*), especially for Sunni Muslims, and the birth of Muslim saints. *Mawalid* (plural of *mawlid*) can be found in greater number among Sunni Muslims. Shiite Muslims remember the martyrdom of Hussein, the grandson of the prophet Muhammad, on the 10th day of Muharram, the first month of the Muslim calendar, and celebrate other great religious figures.

Both Muslim branches have other regular religious celebrations of regional or local importance. For Iran and Kurdistan, a special celebration should be mentioned. It is called Nou-ruz (New Year). It has pre-Islamic origins, and therefore the religious authorities in Iran are critical of it.

But the powers of the Islamic Republic of Iran can not deter Iranians from holding this feast once a year. For the Kurdish nation, which is still struggling for a national home, Nou-ruz has been even more important. To celebrate this day is a sign of national conscience and identity. In the Kurdish areas of Turkey, Iran, or Iraq, authorities tried and still try to hinder Kurds from joining and feasting on that day, with little success. Kurds in the European and American diaspora celebrate Nou-ruz with demonstrations to demand national independence, but also with dancing and eating. For Christians, there are, of course, Christmas and Easter, but also in September the Feast of the Cross (*id al-salib*) and a great number of other celebrations in remembrance of Christian saints. Jews celebrate all Jewish holidays, such as Hanukkah, Yom Kippur, and Passover.

Apart from these regular holidays, the Near and Middle Eastern and North African societies celebrate rites of passage such as circumcisions, baptisms, and bar mitzvahs, which have a religious connotation, and marriage or burial, where the social aspects are stronger. Under normal political circumstances it is sometimes still a custom to accept congratulations not only within one's own religious community, but also from the members of the other two religions. All these celebrations are characterized by (among other things) eating, in some cases special dishes, and these and others in greater quantities. Mostly the females of a family have to do even more work than usual. As it is a custom to visit each other on big holidays, the quantity of food must be even greater than on normal days, and the work to prepare it is, too.

Kuskus Bi-Lahm Wa-Fawakih (Couscous with Lamb and Dried Fruit)

- 1 lb. (500 grams) fine couscous
- 1 lb. (500 grams) lamb stew meat
- 1 onion
- 8 dried apricots
- 2 tbsp. raisins
- 8 dried plums
- 3 tbsp. olive oil
- 1 lemon
- 1 tbsp. butter
- 1 tbsp. brown sugar
- 1 bunch fresh mint
- salt and pepper

Soak the dried fruits in warm water for 30 min., then drain them. Cover the couscous in a strainer with hot water and put it aside. Peel the onion and cut it into strips. Cut the meat in pieces. Heat 2 tbsp. olive oil in a pot and fry the meat for a short time. Add salt and pepper. Add onion and dried fruits. Mix the combination well. Place the strainer with couscous onto the pot and let the meat simmer for about 30 min. If necessary, add water. Now and then, separate the couscous with a fork. If the couscous is ready, place it on a warmed flat bowl and mix it with butter. Place the meat onto it and serve the liquid separately. Wash the lemon with hot water, drain it, and cut it into slices. Pour the rest of the oil into a pan with the brown sugar and let the slices of lemon simmer with it for a short time. Wash the mint and drain it. Take the small leaves and cut them finely. Use the lemons slices and the mint for decoration.

MUSLIM HOLIDAYS

For Muslims, the most important holiday is the holy month of fasting, Ramadan, and the end of this month, the two- or three-day festival of *id al-fitr*. During the whole month, pious Muslims refrain from food and drink (and some other activities) during the day. Exempted are sick persons, pregnant women, small children, travelers, and fighters in the *jihad* (holy war). Muslims are proud to be able to suffer through the fasting, which is hard, especially during the hot period of the year. Children start fasting at the age of seven or eight years for one day only. Later they will participate for longer periods. After they have reached puberty, it is their religious duty to follow the rules of fasting for the whole month. If they have completed the fast for the first time, they are congratulated and receive a present. After sunset, Muslims can break the fast. By tradition this is done with three dates, following the example of the prophet Muhammad, and dates also play an important role in many other dishes during the fasting period. Others eat first some fresh fruit such as apples, oranges, melons, or figs, cut into small pieces. After having eaten that, they might go to the mosque for the evening prayer and return for the real breaking of the fast, which is called Iftar.

There are many different recipes for fast-breaking dishes. Some of them are even named after the Ramadan. There is on the Arab peninsula, for example, a dish called *ramadaniyya*. Apricot paste as well as dried apricots, figs, and plums are soaked overnight in water. The skin of almonds and pistachios is removed. The soaked fruits are mixed with the apricot paste, almonds, pistachios, pine nuts, and orange water. It is a dessert, but may be served as a breaker of the fast. In North Africa, the famous *harira* soup is prepared for the beginning of every meal during Ramadan. It is a combination of lamb broth, lamb, lentils, chickpeas, tomatoes, onions, garlic, fresh herbs, and spices. In the last minutes before serving, the soup can be thickened with flour or yeast. Often it is sprinkled with some fresh lemon or citron juice. During Ramadan, this strengthening soup is put on to the table the minute the end of fasting is announced by the *muezzin* (mosque announcer) or some young men walking through the streets with drums and a kind of trumpet. Today, almost everywhere, the radio or TV also announces "the sign for taking the first spoon." Other small dishes are offered, such as fresh dates, dried figs, and hard-boiled eggs.

Traditionally, the *harira* soup is scooped from a big bowl into small bowls of earthenware and eaten with special spoons made of citron wood with long, slim handles. Of course, there are variations, according to the region or city and even to the time of the year. If the fasting of Ramadan has to be held in the hot summer period, the *harira* can be more light than in winter. In that case, it can be made without meat and with some herbs and spices that are said to be healthy, such as caraway, mastic, and watercress. For a special Tunisian *harira*, little pieces of lamb, chicken

Making doughnuts for Ramadan, Teouan, Morocco. © Art Directors/TRIP Helene Rogers.

intestines, cut onions, lentils, chickpeas, turmeric, cinnamon, ginger, and saffron are cooked together in water; the foam is skimmed off; and the cooking continues for about two hours. At the same time, rice is cooked and, when ready, added to the soup. At the end, yeast is mixed with hot water, tomatoes, coriander, and parsley; added to the soup; and cooked together for another 15 minutes. The *harira* should be served very hot. Every housewife has her special combination of ingredients for this soup. One uses more meat, but in very small pieces; another uses more lentils and chickpeas; and others add the hot *harisa* sauce just before serving. Today the *harira* soup is also offered outside the month of Ramadan, mostly in hotels and restaurants. With families it continues to be a typical Ramadan dish.

In Turkey and among the Turkish diaspora in western Europe, the soup for breaking the fast is a tripe soup called *ishkembe corbasi*. As it is, today, more complicated to prepare it at home, in Istanbul or other big Turkish cities one can buy it in special shops or in huts where it is offered only during Ramadan. For this soup, the tripe has to be cleaned and put into a pan and covered with water, which is brought to a boil. The froth is skimmed off, and the tripe is cooked until tender—about 20 minutes. Then the tripe is taken out of the cooking liquid and dried and cut into small slices. Then a roux of butter and flour is made, and the tripe liquid is added, stirring always until it is slightly thickened. The tripe is added and simmers for 15 minutes. In a second pot, an egg yolk is beaten with lemon juice and a little of the hot liquid from the soup. Then all is poured into the soup and stirred vigorously to avoid curdling. Salt and fresh-ground black pepper should be added. The quantity of salt is important, because of the fasting, especially in summertime. The *ishkembe corbasi* is spiced or garnished with a special mixture of white-wine vinegar, some garlic cloves (sometimes soaked in the vinegar), crushed salt, and some sharp pickles. This soup in Turkey is often served with a special bread called *ramazan pide*. *Pide* are soft bread pouches. This large, round or oval, hollowed, spongy bread is served to soak up all kinds of more liquid food. In Ramadan, sesame seeds are sprinkled on top. Some people tear the *ramazan pide* into pieces and put it into the soup.

In Iran, the breaking of the fast is also done with some special dishes. In the northern and central parts, the fasting is broken with a soup of milk and rice, rice flour, or saffron rice. Another way of opening the Iftar meal is by the traditional dates and some sweets. The most common in the south of the country is called *sulbiya*. For that, yogurt and starch are stirred together, and saffron, flour, and baking powder are added, so that a dough of a creamy but firm consistency develops. This is set aside for about two hours. During that period, sugar, lemon juice, rose water, and honey are mixed with water and cooked for about 20 minutes until it has become a syrup. In a deep pot, oil is heated. Then doughnuts are formed and fried in the hot oil. They will sink down first and rise to the surface when they are done. Then they are taken out of the oil, dipped into the syrup, and put aside until they are cool.

The Iftar meal excels in both quality and quantity. The whole spectrum of the cuisine of the Near and Middle East and North Africa is put on the table. There are sometimes games connected with these meals. A pearl may be mixed into rice, which can be kept by the happy one who finds it. Before the beginning of the next day, when the fasting again starts, there is an early-morning meal called *sahur* for which, traditionally, young men walk through the city streets knocking on the doors to wake up the sleepers. Normally it is a light meal, because people think that a heavy meal will make them thirsty during the day and thus add to the hardships of fasting. At the end of Ramadan, the young men receive a little gift of money or food for their job during this month.

The breaking of the fast also has very strong social and political aspects. During this period it is customary to visit each other. Relatives, friends, and neighbors go to each other's houses and are invited for Iftar, the breaking of the fast. There are certain rules for these visits. Parents have to be visited by their children—first the older ones, and then the younger. Brothers and sisters visit each other, also according to age. All visits have to be answered by another visit the other way around, so that the parents will visit their children. These visits also function to solve personal problems that have arisen during the last year between family members. Within a neighborhood, visiting rituals are much easier, as there are often very close personal contacts. As in some countries, today not all Muslims are keeping the fast. Neighbors know who is following the rules, and there is an exchange of food in the evening between those who are fasting. For important political persons, from the president of the republic to the mayor of a town or the headman of a village, it is obligatory to invite, every evening, a group of people to break the fast with them. These guests can be invited according to their function or social or political role, so perhaps on one evening university teachers are invited to join the head of state for the Iftar, on another evening a group of officers, on still another diplomats, and so on.

Political parties and charity organizations also organize Iftar events. For example, in a certain quarter of a city, it is announced that this party or that organization invites people for Iftar. Long tables and chairs are put on the street, and after the call of the *muezzin*, members of the organization serve their guests, who are often from the poorer strata of this quarter. It may be that before the meal, some parts of the Quran are recited or a prayer is offered together. In some cases it may be, especially if religious charity organizations are offering the food, that a preacher gives a sermon, which is normally quite short, because everybody is hungry and will not pay great attention to his words. Newspapers and TV news will inform the public about the people who are invited to the president's house as well as about the organizations that prepared an Iftar table. For politicians an Iftar party is an occasion to communicate with their followers and show themselves as pious Muslims. Parties and charitable organizations can show their abilities of action, find sympathizers, and gain a following.

As fasting is the center of the Ramadan, food is also quite central. The many Ramadan specialties require special ingredients, which increase in price during that time. Political and religious authorities criticize this practice, and newspapers comment with caricatures on the darker side of Ramadan.

The second great holiday for Muslims is the Feast of Sacrifice, by which Muslims commemorate the sacrifice of Abraham, who was ready to kill his only son, Ishmael (by the Muslim tradition), who was rescued by an angel who substituted him with a lamb. This feast takes place during the time of the big pilgrimage to the holy city of Mecca and between the 10th and 12th of the month, called Dhu l-Hijja. Not only the pilgrims in Mecca but all Muslims in the world slaughter an animal on that day, one per family. What animal is slaughtered depends on the economic situation of the family. Poor ones will only kill a chicken or a dove. More affluent families have a lamb. The animal is eaten right after the slaughtering. Mostly the more fleshy parts are grilled; others are cooked, and the intestines are also used. But there are no special recipes for this occasion. Rich families slaughter several lambs or a big animal like a cow or a camel and distribute what they cannot consume to the poor. In Turkey, this feast is called *seker bayrami* (sugar feast). This indicates that there are special sweets for the children. In Egypt and in North Africa, on the Feast of Sacrifice people will visit the graves of deceased relatives. They will spend some time there and have a picnic. What is not eaten is left on the gravestones when the family leaves the place in the evening. In the past there was the tradition that the dead persons could not eat the food but could smell it. Today, the explanation for this custom is that poor people of the city should have the chance to take that food.

On the days of the commemoration of the birth of famous and of less famous Muslims saints (*mawlid*) on their burying places, there are rituals that also involve food. Compared with the great Muslim holidays, a *mawlid* has a stronger social than family character. Only on the occasion of the *mawlid al-nabi*, the birthday of the prophet Muhammad, do children receive some sweets. The rituals take place in mosques and near the burying places of the saints. Many of the rituals in connection with these commemorations follow certain rules, which also involve food. There are prayers that can last for hours. And it is the task of some of the commemorators to see that food and water or juice are given to the praying believers when there is a short interval. The same can be said of the meetings of Islamic mystics (Sufi) who are also practicing long rituals. The food that is offered is normally sweets, like one called *halqum* made from starch, sugar, mastic, and pistachios. One could call it an energy food because it gives strength to the praying. Again, on the occasion of these *mawlid* feasts, especially religious Muslim organizations such as the mystic brotherhoods, which have their centers all over the Muslim world and nowadays also in western Europe and North America, prepare tents near the graves of the saints and entertain the visitors with food and drink. The different brotherhoods compete in the quality, decoration, and luxury of their tents, and also in the quality and quantity of the food and nonalcoholic drinks they offer to the visitors. This is done because of charity, but also to attract young people to their respective brotherhood. There may be special recipes for certain *mawlid* feasts, but generally sweets and pickled vegetables are offered, because of problems of transportation and keeping the food fresh.

Shiite Islam is characterized by higher emotions than the Sunni version of this religion. Mourning for the great figures in Shiite religious history is central to the ritual. The highest feast is the mourning for the martyrdom of Hussein, the grandson of prophet Muhammad. This takes place on the 10th day of the Muslim month of Muharram, which is the first month of the Islamic year. This day is called Ashura. Its rituals are passion plays, in which the history of the death of Hussein is reenacted, and ceremonies in which young men in groups wander through the Shiite cities and Shiite quarters of big cities flagellating themselves with whips and iron chains and even using swords or big knives that they beat against their forehead while expressing ritualistic words of grief. The nine days before are also days of sorrow and grief, when the historical development leading to the death of Hussein is recited over and over. These recitations can take place in meetings in private homes, especially if they are organized by and for women. The hostess of such a gathering will pay the specialists who re-cite the story of Hussein and will see that there is food and drink for her guests. Normally these are only simple dishes, water, and some sweets. For Shiite women, these meeting have a highly social importance, besides the religious side. These are occasions where they can meet, exchange information, organize marriages, and much more. For the passion plays, which can last hours, the organizers see to it that the spectators can have water and little snacks, which are sold by persons who are working for the organizing institution or on their own account. The only specialty that is used during Ashura is *halqum* (see previous paragraph), which is given by accompanying helpers to the flagellators during their rituals.

Forty days after Ashura, there is another celebration that also com-memorates the death of important persons in Shiite Islam history. This day is called Arba'in, which means "forty" in Arabic. In Iraq, Shiite shep-herds collect the milk of their flock for this period and prepare butter or cheese from it, which they give away as alms to the needy.

For Sunni Muslims, Ashura is also a day of grief, which they commemo-rate by fasting. But until the early 1980s, in North Africa Ashura had a completely different character. It was like a carnival. Students elected their sultan, who for that day even had political power in some cities on Morocco such as Fez or Marrakech. Children on that day, even today, beg for sweets, and if they are refused they pour water over the greedy. There are also rituals with fire. For example, a vertical wooden pole is erected, with wood and fuel put at the base. A fire is lit, and after a while the pole will fall to one side. The direction of its fall indicates the quality of the harvest.

The North African Ashura also has a special dish. This consists of slices of veal filled with seven special green herbs and made into a roll that is fried in fat.[1] The herbs and vegetables are leeks; cilantro; parsley; mint; and, depending on the season, wild green asparagus, artichokes, and fen-nel. There are also special cakes in the shape of a fish or other animal. During the Middle Ages, these cakes could be found in many parts of the Muslim world, even in the holy city of Mecca. In Morocco during the French colonial period, the question arose of whether this was allowed because of the religious prohibition of painting or forming the pictures of animals or human beings. A special religious ruling allowed these shapes for cakes.[2]

The peak of Iranian holiday culture is Nou-ruz (Persian for "New Year"). It starts in the moment of the equinox when the sun enters the astronomi-cal sign of the ram. Tradition says that this is the time when the earth, which is rotating on the top of one horn of a two-horned bull, moves from one horn-top to the other. The holiday is traditionally declared by Haji Firuz, a clown in red clothes and a darkened face, singing and dancing along the streets and collecting money in his special cone-shaped hat. On that occasion, only presents of money are allowed. The house should be cleaned, and it is an occasion to buy new clothes. The Nou-ruz feast lasts for 13 days. For the feast, a table is set with seven items starting with the letter s. These can be taken from food words as well—for example, serkeh (vinegar, a symbol of conservation), sir (garlic, said to improve the health), sabzeh (wheat grass, a sign of the new life), sumakh (sumac), sib (apple), or sendshed (the fruit of hawthorn). Other things also have a symbolic value. It is said that there is a little trembling when the bull throws the world from one horn to the other. The trembling changes the position of the seven items on the table. This is also the case with eggs, which are placed on a flat mirror on that occasion. From that moving, one can read what the next year will bring. The last day of Nou-ruz, the 13th, bears some risks, because in Iranian tradition the number 13 means bad luck. The family will clean the table with the seven items and wander to a stream or river, where the green wheat grains are thrown into the water, carrying away all misfortune. This is also the occasion for a picnic, followed by dancing and singing.

A typical dish of Nou-ruz is the *shekar polo*. This is an old recipe, already known by about 1500 in Iran.[3] It is made from pieces of chicken, chickpeas, cinnamon, rice, and pistachios. When the rice is ready, sugar syrup is added. Another rice dish that is eaten on Nou-ruz is *alo-balo polo*. For this, morello cherries are cooked with sugar in a pot until the cherries start to become tender and most of the juice has come out. After that the pot is put aside. Then a chicken is washed, dried, and salted inside and out. In hot olive oil, the chicken is browned without burning. The chicken is put aside, and onions are roasted in the remaining oil. The chicken is returned to the pot without any liquid. Water is added, the pot is covered well, and cooking continues until the chicken is very tender. It is taken aside and, when cooled down a little, cut into six to eight pieces. In another pot, water is heated, and then rice is added to the water in a way that does not stop the cooking. Cooking should continue for five minutes. Then the rice is put through a large sieve. Then some of the broth of the chicken and some melted butter is put into the still-hot pot. One-half of the rice is added. The cook should work with a spoon to bring the rice to all sides of the pot, so that one has a complete surface. This is steamed for five minutes on medium heat. Then the pot is taken off the heat. The pieces of chicken are spread on the rice equally. Then half of the cooked cherries are added. This all is covered with the other half of the rice, and next with the rest of the cherries. Then the pot is tightly lidded, and cooking continues for 15 minutes, until the rice is ready. But the preparation is still not finished. A cup of the cooked rice is taken out and is mixed with some melted butter and saffron that is soaking in water. After some stirring, the rice should shine and be a dark yellow color. On a large plate, the upper part of the rice is spread, and the chicken pieces are put on top, covered with the rest of the rice. Onto that the yellow saffron rice is sprinkled. There is always some rice at the bottom of the pot that has become very crispy. It is called the "heart" of the rice. This is loosened with a spatula. If it comes out of the pot as a whole, it is broken into pieces and put around the sides of the plate. This is a very colorful and delicate dish.

As a typical Kurdish kitchen has not yet been identified, it is difficult to report on Kurdish Nou-ruz dishes, but Kurds also have picnics near rivers and dance and have fun. Some regimes that dominate the Kurdish regions understand this as a political demonstration of Kurdish national pride, and so these activities are watched closely by the authorities.

JEWISH HOLIDAYS

Compared with Muslims, Jews have more holidays, and with these more special culinary practices. Rosh Hashanah, New Year's Day, is the first feast. Like the Muslim Feast of Sacrifice, it remembers the sacrifice of Abraham. On that day, Jews pray that the coming year should be sweet as honey and apple, so it is not surprising that sweet dishes are offered to the family on that day. There is in Morocco, for example, vegetables with sugar. Chickpeas and beans are soaked overnight in a big pot, and many small onions (cut into quarters) and pieces of lamb (preferably of the head of a sheep or other kind of less expensive meat) are added with water and cooked. After one hour other vegetables such as turnips and zucchini are added. What is used depends the region. Mustard, quite a quantity of sugar, salt, and some cinnamon are added. This dish is served apart from the other dishes, and the eldest should serve every person around the table a spoon of it with a prayer. Another recipe used on that day is prepared with quince. The fruit is peeled and cut into quarters. Then the same quantity of fruit and sugar and some cinnamon is put into a pot, covered with water, and cooked until the water has evaporated and the fruit turns red. On one day of the two-day feast holiday, fish should also be served.

Yom Kippur is a day of fasting, prayer, confession, and repentance. Among the North African Jewry, the day was also called the Feast of Chicken. It was said that for each male in the family a cock should be slaughtered, and for each female a pullet. The chicken dishes were eaten before the fasting started in the evening. One typical recipe is chicken with onions. For that, cooked chicken pieces are added to onions and saffron cooked in oil, seasoned with salt and pepper.

Sukut is the Jewish thanksgiving. It lasts for seven days, and food is always plentiful. For this holiday, nougat with almonds is typical. Purim, the holiday that remembers the heroine Esther, can be compared with the Christian carnival, when children dress up. For the adults, the drinking of one or more glasses of wine is not unusual. Hanukkah is the holiday that remembers the reconquest of Jerusalem. Central to the holiday ritual is the lightning of the menorah, so it can be called a feast of light. Oil plays an important role, and oily dishes are preferable. But North African Jews also have their own special recipe. It is fish with carrots.

At Passover, the big holiday that lasts one week, Jews remember the exodus of the Children of Israel from Egypt. It is a feast of joy and prosperity. Passover can be described as a family feast. Typical all over the Jewish world is matzo, an unleavened bread. In the different Jewish communities of North Africa there many special recipes. A Tunisian specialist describes some of the dishes of the Jews of Tunisia. "On the first two days of the feast of Pessah the table was dressed lavishly like it should be: 'M'soki', a ragout of spring vegetables and 'Osben.'" Osben is a kind of a sausage made of intestines, which are cooked for a short time and then chopped together with spinach, parsley, and garlic. This is mixed with the North African hot allspice harisa, uncooked rice, leaves of coriander and mint, salt, and pepper. All this is mixed thoroughly and filled into the skin, so that one has one or more sausages. Half an hour before the end of cooking, it can be given to a dish. The m'soki consists of veal meat, new onions, tomatoes, garlic, spinach, green peas, a young white cabbage, some fresh turnips, fresh carrots, a clod of fennel, some celery, some bottoms of artichokes, fresh fava beans, leaves of coriander and mint, matzo, olive oil, salt, and pepper. The meat in small pieces is fried with onions and tomatoes, and then the rest of the vegetables are added according to the duration of cooking of the different ingredients. The time for cooking is about three to four hours on very low heat. The last added ingredients should be the bottoms of the artichokes and the leaves of coriander and mint. The osben can be cooked with the vegetables, but should be removed 15 minutes before the end of cooking. Before serving, broken matzo is crumbled.[4]

The regular Jewish feast of the week is, of course, Shabbat (Sabbath). It starts on Friday night and lasts until Saturday evening. As it is (among other things) not allowed for Jews to light a fire, special recipes had to be developed to overcome this prohibition. One of the North African Shabbat dishes has the name *skhina* (heated) or *dfina* (buried). One needs a big piece of veal, minced meat in a quarter of the quantity of the veal, a foot of a young calf, hard-boiled eggs, peeled potatoes, chickpeas, rice or wheat, onions, salted water, a date or some sugar or honey to sweeten the dish, oil, pepper, and some more water. There is a special technique for arranging the different ingredients in layers. First come the chickpeas, then the onions and the date, and then the pieces of meat are put into a corner of the big pot that is needed for this dish. Then the potatoes follow. All this is sprinkled with some oil, covered with water, and cooked. After one hour, the minced meat is prepared and formed into a ball that is wrapped into a piece of mousseline. The same is done with the rice. The boiled eggs and the balls with minced meat and rice are put into the pot, and cooking water is added if necessary. Then the pot is left on the fire, which is going to burn down overnight, or it is brought to the public oven until the next day. The food simmers on the lowest heat for 18 to 24 hours. Today one can use electric chafing dishes that keep the food warm and that require no switching on or off or regulating. The way of serving the *skhina* is also special. On one plate the eggs, potatoes, and rice or wheat are placed. On a second plate comes the meat. The chickpeas are brought on still on other plate. The sauce is served in a sauce boat.

CHRISTIAN HOLIDAYS

The Christian faith in the Near and Middle East and North Africa is very much divided into several older and modern denominations. As Christians since the beginning of modernity have been under a strong influence from Western culture, many European customs for religious holidays are practiced. This is especially the case with Christmas, when Christmas trees are found everywhere. Turkey is also the traditional meat on Christmas in the Near and Middle East and North Africa. However, the food that is prepared during the Lenten period before Easter is more resistant to foreign influences. Most of the Christian churches have strong fasting regulations. During the fasts before Easter, in some branches, all animal products and fish are forbidden, with milk there are some exceptions. On Wednesday and Friday, oil and wine are also forbidden. These prohibitions are also valid for the Passion Week. During that week a meal may consist of beans, potatoes, green salad, onions, olives, and water. Only halvah, a sweet dish made of sugar, milk, oil, and semolina, gives a special culinary accent to this quite-frugal meal.

On Easter, of course, lamb is on the table. Normally it is roasted whole on a spit. A special treat for guests is the grilled lamb liver. For that, the liver is washed and rinsed, cut into pieces, and coated in wheat flour. It is fried quickly in very hot olive oil. The liver should not become hard. The pieces are put into a bowl and salted and peppered. Young onions and parsley are added.

Easter is the time when many different kinds of sweets are prepared. One of them is the famous *baklawa* (baklava), made of walnuts and/or pistachios, sugar, butter, and phyllo dough, bought fresh or frozen. Other ingredients are honey, lemon juice, cinnamon, and rose or orange-flower water. The dough and the nut mixture are alternately layered. The secret to preparing these sweets is now retained largely only by elderly house-wives. Today most families buy *baklawa* in special shops.

Samak Bi-L-Tahina (Fish with *Tahîna* Sauce)

- 1 flat fish (flounder or halibut), about 2 lbs. (1 kg)
- 2 tbsp. lemon juice
- 2 cloves crushed garlic
- 1 tbsp. olive oil
- salt and pepper
- 3/4 cup (200 ml) *tahîna* (tahini paste)
- 2 cloves crushed garlic
- 4 tbsp. lemon juice
- water
- salt

Clean and scale the fish, leaving the head and tail intact. Rub the fish with lemon juice, garlic, oil, salt, and pepper. Bake the fish for about 20 min. in an oven at 350 degrees (180°C). Chill and then remove the skin and bones carefully. If using a whole fish, rearrange the head and the tail by remolding into a fish shape. Keep it warm, not hot. Now prepare the *tahîna* sauce by adding water and lemon juice alternately until it is thick. (The water thins and the lemon juice thickens the *tahîna*.) Add garlic, pepper, and salt. Coat the body of the molded fish with the *tahîna* sauce and smooth it with a spatula, leaving the head and tail uncovered. If desired, garnish it with lightly fried pine nuts, sprigs of coriander, and parsley.

LIFE-CYCLE CELEBRATIONS

As in many traditional societies, the birth of a child is connected with many beliefs and rituals. For women in traditional Near and Middle Eastern and North African societies, it is important to bear many children. Barrenness is very bad luck. So some rituals involve the use of food to help bring on a pregnancy. An Iranian folklorist described one as follows: "On the last Wednesday before the Iranian New Year, a woman will take seven walnuts, seven almond, seven leek leaves, and seven colored threads. She will break the walnuts and the almonds and scatter them with the leek leaves upon the ground for others to pick them up and eat. She will tie the threads to her great toe and then cut them. This procedure is considered effective in producing pregnancy."[5] When pregnant, among other rituals, the woman should eat camel flesh and wear a tiny bag containing garlic skin, salt crystal, and seeds of wild rue (an evergreen shrub). As pregnant women are often afraid of the evil eye or malevolent ghosts, they use talismans and other devices to avert them. Among the aids against evil forces are herbs such as the wild rue, which can be hung in the bedroom where mother and child are sleeping.[6]

As birthing is a tiring process, special dishes are prepared for the mother. Most dishes are for strengthening. At the same time, these dishes should not be too heavy. Often a soup or a dish made from eggs is brought to the young mother by the midwives or a neighbor. On that occasion, in North Africa, a little garlic, cumin, salt, tomato pulp, and perhaps the hot allspice *harira* are mixed with water and fried in olive oil. More water is added, and some dried mint leaves are crumbled and added. Fresh eggs are scrambled and put into the soup. Some bread can be toasted, and the soup is poured over it. In Iran, the mother is fed rice with milk, or, if she is from a more affluent family, a rice soup with milk, saffron, almonds, and other ingredients. While the soup is eaten mainly by the laboring woman, the rice is prepared in great quantities and also eaten by the women who assist and some of the guests, particularly the children, who come to congratulate the new mother.

After delivery, certain food rules have to be observed so that the mother regains her strength. A special dish is prepared on the fourth day after the delivery. A rooster and a hen are cooked together. On the 5th and 10th days, the young mother will have bread, fried eggs, and a thick soup that is heavy with grease. During the first nine days she is not allowed to eat vegetables or fruit; only melons are an exemption during the season. On the 10th day she may drink a vegetable soup. In some countries on the Arab peninsula, a newborn child is carried by the mother around the house while his or her young brothers and sisters or any other children hold burning candles. The newborn is introduced to the house and its inhabitants in this way. For their service, the children get some sweets or fruit.

Muslim boys are circumcised between the ages of 1 and 11 or 12. This is an occasion for a great feast for relatives and friends. The boys receive presents such as clothes, toys, or sweets. A comparable rite of passage in Jewish communities is the bar mitzvah, or the first holy communion in the Christian communities. Families serve a big meal with many different dishes. But there are no special recipes for these occasions. From that celebration onward, the Jewish or Christian boys are allowed to drink a sip of alcohol, especially wine.

From a culinary point of view, these feasts are not very interesting. Weddings are a different story. Weddings in the Near and Middle East and North Africa are still the domain of the women of the family. In traditional families, the women choose the wife for a son who wants to get married. Of course, they will do it in such a way that the men have the impression that they are the ones who actually finally decide. One of the criteria for the women in choosing a bride who will come into their house is her ability to help and later organize on her own the various duties that have to be fulfilled by her in the household. So, along with character, education, and looks, it is important that she know how to cook. Potential brides are visited by female relatives of a possible husband. It is the special duty of the young women to serve her possible in-laws with pastries that are prepared (or said to be prepared) by herself.

Later, when the women have decided that the young woman would be suitable for the young man and for the women of the household, the men start the official negotiations over the marriage contract. If the deliberations are successful, in many traditional societies of the Near and Middle East and North Africa, the groom's family will send gifts to the family of the bride-to-be. One gift is always sugar, a symbol of the good relations between the two families that could begin with this marriage. The marriage contract can deal with many different topics, even the type of kitchen and appliances she will have. This contract is presented at the Islamic court and taken into the official records. The bridegroom, bride, a male representative of the bride, and two witnesses are present when the contract is presented. The bride is asked if she agrees to the marriage. If she does not respond, this is taken as approval, because it is assumed that she is too shy to answer in the presence of men she does not know. This is the central marriage ceremony. In Iran, after that, wild rue is burned. By this the evil eye is cast off. Seeds of wild rue are also used in a dish that is prepared for the guests: "It is believed that these seeds are hallowed by being with the food at a wedding feast, and that thus magic may be done with them."[7]

Some time after that, another feast takes place. This can be shortly afterward, but also some months or even years later. This depends on the economic situation, but today, it can also happen if the young couple finds their own apartment. During this feast, the bride is brought from her parental home to her new home with the family of her husband. Here she is received by the women of her new home with milk, sweets, and almonds, food that has highly symbolical value. Milk is a sign of affluence as well as virginity, but also of fertility; sweets and almonds indicate that the young woman is welcomed by her new female relatives. Dates are also offered. This transfer of the bride is celebrated by eating and drinking, as well as dancing and rejoicing. Here again the great quantity of food is an important aspect.

In North Africa, the preparations of the actual rite of passage can take seven days and is a feast of its own, although it is combined with lots of preparation for the women of the household. A part of that takes place in the house of the bride. The most important day is the last one, called "henna night." The bride, dressed in white and green clothes, sits in the middle of a room surrounded by other women. At her feet are plates with sugar, cloves, eggs, and milk. There are also plates with henna, which is a green herb, which is crushed and processed and will give a red color; dried rose flowers; and incense. The last is to avert evil spirits. A female specialist will decorate the hands, feet, and cheeks of the bride with the henna in very complicated designs. This takes hours, because the color needs time to dry. If there is enough time and the design should remain for a longer time, the hands and feet are wrapped in cloth for several hours or even a day. Some of the henna is eaten by the designer and by the bride. It is said that for them it tastes good. All the other women present are also prepared with henna, although the design for them is less elaborate. A female hairdresser will then start fixing the bride's hair.

During these hours, the other women sit around, singing, joking, drinking many glasses of tea with mint, eating cookies and pastries (which are offered all over again), and dancing to the rhythm of the drums they are playing. The sweets are *ghoriba, kaab al-ghazal,* and *briouat.* The *ghoriba* is a cookie made of powdered sugar, almonds, an egg, crushed citron peel, inner seeds of vanilla bean, and cinnamon. The egg and the powdered sugar are mixed, the ground almonds and the other ingredients are added, and a dough is prepared and set aside for a quarter of an hour. Then little balls are flattened and formed like coins. These are baked for 20 minutes and then sprinkled with powdered sugar.

Kaab al-ghazal means "horn of a gazelle." For this pastry, a dough is made from wheat flour, melted butter, egg yolk, orange-flower water, and some water. The dough should have the consistency of bread dough. The dough is formed into a ball and set aside. Then the almond filling is prepared. Almonds, sugar, and orange-flower water are creamed in a blender. Then an egg is added. The dough is rolled into flat layers and cut into several small sections. These are filled with the almond cream while spread, and then rolled up and put into a medium-hot stove for about 20 minutes.

Briouat is a pastry made of very thin dough leaves, which can be filled with salty as well as sweet fillings. For a wedding they are sweet, naturally. Sweet fillings may be made of rice with orange-flower water and cinnamon. There is also a recipe with the filling made of crushed peanuts, orange-flower water, powdered sugar, butter, and cinnamon.

These cookies and pastries are prepared also for other occasions, but for big weddings they are made in enormous quantities. With the quantities of sweets needed only for the henna night, all the guests bring their share, and the women will compete to see who brings the most delicious ones. The night before the wedding feast, friends of the bridegroom will accompany him to the public bath. This separation of gender in traditional families will continue during most of the feast. Men and women will eat and celebrate in different rooms. Only at the end, when the bride and groom come together, are they accompanied to their room by the male and female family members and guests. But in general, it is the older generation who is present on that occasion.

When the bride and the groom come together first during this feast, he will feed her a date and some milk, and she will do likewise for him. In an Afghan wedding, a soup is brought before the young couple and they have to feed each other, each one having a spoon. In Morocco, with all the preparations it may be well into midnight before dinner.

All over the Near and Middle East and North Africa, there are more dishes that are typical for such an occasion. There is, for instance, the famous Turkish *düğün çorbasi* (marriage soup). It is a soup made of lamb meat. Another Turkish wedding dish is a lamb ragout. Moroccan wedding dishes include *bstilla*, made from dove, lamb, couscous, almonds, and raisins, and a special chicken preparation called *dajaj miharomas*.

In many Near and Middle Eastern and North African societies, there is one rule during the meal: that the gifts given to the young couple are announced loudly. The guests bring many different things—jewelry, household goods, money, and also food that is consumed during the wedding feast. There is a strong law of reciprocity in these traditional societies, and everybody feels obliged to return gifts of an equal value on another occasion. Also, if a family is confronted with a sudden economic crisis and cannot return what they have received before, prepared food is an interesting gift. Normally, the whole community knows about the problems. In that case not only the costs of the ingredients can be rated, but also the experience and the efforts of the producer. If the family has recovered economically after a time, they are expected to go back to the normal ways of gift exchange.

Many modern Near and Middle Eastern and North African upper-middle-class urban families today prefer to hold wedding feasts in the ballroom or reception rooms of big international hotels. Here the gender separation will not be very consequential, as families are sitting together and the young couple is placed on a throne at the center of the room. There is always live music and dancers. The presentation of the wedding gifts plays a minor role. As the celebration is quite a formal social event, the question of food is also of less importance. The menu has regional and Western dishes prepared by the hotel kitchen. The event is often crowned by sparkling ice-cream bombs, which are carried by a line of waiters into the darkened ballroom. The other possibility is a buffet. The couple will cut a piece out of a multilayered wedding cake and feed each other.

The last rite of passage is death and burial. As Muslim customs demand that the corpse be buried as soon as possible after the death and should stay in the house overnight only if the person passed away late in the evening, and certain rituals, such as ablutions, have to be performed before the burial, there is no time for food customs. But after the burial, there is an official period of mourning, during which the Quran is read for the soul of the deceased. This is also a time when visitors come to offer their condolences to those left behind. The visitors should be fed. This is thought good for the soul of the dead. Again the traditional sweets are offered. In some regions, a thick soup may be served. In traditional communities there is the conviction that the soul of the dead will roam around for some time and try to return to his or her home. The traditions last anywhere from 7 to 40 days. Magic charms are used to hinder the coming back of the soul. At the end of the period, the family of the dead should have a meal for all relatives, neighbors, friends, and other persons near to the dead who have time to come. If this meal is not organized, it is believed that the dead may become angry with the family and do them harm. In the rare case that a person has no family left when dying, he or she will see to it that there is some money for such a meal that can be organized by someone.[8]

NOTES

1. Outside the Near and Middle East and North Africa, but among Muslims, there are other food rituals connected with Ashura. For example, in Malaysia it is, like in North Africa, a day of feasting and is said to commemorate a day when the prophet Muhammad had nothing special to eat, so he tossed everything at hand into a pot and cooked the lot. See Raymond Firth, "Cooking in a Kelantan Fishing Village," in *The Anthropologist Cookbook*, ed. J. Kuper (London: Macmillan, 1967), 186.

2. Paul Ricard, "Gateaux Berbères," *Hespéris* 6 (1926): 426–29.

3. Bert Fragner, "Zur Erforschung der kulinarischen Kultur Irans," *Die Welt des Islams*, vols. 23, 24 (1984): 359.

4. Odette Touitou, *Tunisie—La cuisine de ma mère* (Geneve: Edition Minerva, 2003), 86–88.

5. Bess Donaldson, *The Wild Rue* (New York: Arno Press, 1938), 24.

6. Donaldson, *Wild Rue*, 27.

7. Donaldson, *Wild Rue*, 51.

8. Hilma Granqvist, *Muslim Death and Burial: Arab Customs and Traditions Studied in a Jordanian Village* (Helsingfors: Soderstorm, 1965).

7

Diet and Health

TRADITIONAL MEDICAL THEORIES ABOUT FOOD

The most important religions of the Near and Middle East and North Africa—Judaism, Christianity, and Islam—have food regulations. This is especially true for Jews and Muslims, whereas the religious laws concerning food for Christians concentrate on rules of fasting. During the last hundred years there have been many discussions about Jewish and Muslim food taboos, and still now one can hear of dietary reasons for the prohibition of pork or wine. The divine wisdom of these taboos is emphasized after modern medicine has detected the negative consequences of excessive consumption of fat.

Although the modern Western medical systems dominate the health ideology and healing methods in most of the countries of the region, there are still explanations for certain dietary rules that have a premodern tradition. Most of them go back to the Hellenic world. During those times, and until quite recently, both the uneducated and the educated and even physicians believed in the humoral system. This system classifies humans, food, and many other things into four different categories: hot, cold, dry, and moist. If these four attributes are in balance in the body of a human, he or she is healthy. If an imbalance develops because of external factors such as climate, stress, or poor nutrition, the result will be sickness. To become healthy again, it is necessary to regain the humoral balance. This can be achieved by food, among other things. If a person is thought to have too much coldness, he or she should eat food that is known to be hot; if he or she is too moist, he or she should eat something dry; and so on.

This system is used today by traditional physicians in the Near and Middle East and North Africa and plays an important role in the traditional folk medicine of the region. However, the humoral system has been simplified over the years. Since the Middle Ages, special books have given exact information about the functions of different foods according to these categories. These multivolume publications are used today. But now, many of these traditional physicians and healers know only the two categories of hot and cold. To give an example: As any kind of sour food like pickles is considered to be cold, it should not be eaten when somebody has a cold. In that case, the cold will become worse.[1] Traditional physicians are very much concerned about colds in general. They are convinced that such a condition may become worse if it is not cured with right diet. To eat without paying attention to what is right or wrong will lead to insanity, because the cold will influence the head of the patient.[2]

Other diseases, such as pneumonia or tuberculosis, are considered to be warm. During the development of a disease, it can also turn from hot to cold or the other way around. So measles, scarlet fever, whooping cough, and smallpox are first cold and later become hot. With these maladies it is much more difficult to find the right way of curing with food. Of course, there are discussions among the specialists about which food is cold. Experts do not agree on whether sour milk is cold or not, because sheep's milk is considered hot. The meat of sheep, camels, hens, ducks, doves, partridges, and turkey hens is hot. Cow's milk is cold, as is the meat from cows, roosters, turkey cocks, and fish. Surprisingly, ice cream is hot. Most nuts are hot. For fruits and vegetables, each one has to be determined separately. Astonishingly, the milk of the mother of a boy baby is considered to be hot, while that of the mother of a girl baby is cold.

Humoral medicine can be considered scientific because it is a complex and logical system that is built on the consequent idea of effects influencing human health. It is a complete theory on the world, which today is old-fashioned, but which has a long history and fascinates modern medical specialists. Beside this, there are other types of healing that cannot be called scientific, because they are not connected with a complete system of thought, but rather pick from various traditions: magical, religious, natural, and many others. In most cases they are influenced by religio-magical traditions. In the Iranian tradition, some recipes may help in difficult medical and social circumstances. One of them is said to have been invented by Fatima, the daughter of prophet Muhammad. She cooked a potful of gruel made from rice, milk, grease, sugar, and cardamom seed. It should be cooked in a dark room without males being present, because they will become blind. Whoever eats from this dish will receive what he or she wishes, especially health. If the wish comes true, one has to pay a reward to the woman who has cooked the gruel.[3] Another healing dish is made of lentils and spinach, the ingredients to be bought with money that is asked for on the street.[4]

Traditional medicine has rules pertaining to eating habits to strengthen the body and help fight illness. For example, children in the Near and Middle East and North Africa are advised how to eat to stay healthy. This advice is often connected with important persons of religious history to enhance its authority. So Ali, the cousin and son-in-law of the prophet Muhammad, is said to have given the following rules to his son, Hassan, to escape the doctors: not to eat until he was very hungry, to leave the table before he was quite satisfied, and to chew his food until it became soft.[5] Another tradition says that one should eat a little bit of salt before and after a meal. If you did, God would exempt you from 72 kinds of ca-lamities, including insanity, cancer, and leprosy. This rule was said to be given by God to Moses. Another often-followed tradition is to drink a sip of vinegar before the meal. This is said to increase intelligence.

In Islamic folk practices, some food items are also used as part of talis-mans, like black beans and other pulses. In Egypt, newborn babies receive little sacks filled with seven various ingredients. They may consist of anis-ette, coriander, nigella, beans, peas, and a kind of wheat or other cereals. This talisman will avert all evil from the child. Beans are also spread on the floor of the room where the delivery takes place. This is also done to soothe whoever may do harm to the child.[6]

The various possession cults of the Near and Middle East and North Africa that also have healing functions are often combined with food and eating. Ghosts who take possession of a person may like certain types of food, and will torment their victims until they get it. Certain kinds of food, items such as incense, or certain colors or melodies are connected with certain ghosts. Obsession-cult specialists can tell which ghost is tor-menting an obsessed person by the food the ghost is demanding. The pos-sessed person will eat the food while still not being conscious. It is likely that the torments of a possessed person will be reduced after that.

Members of obsession cults, which are known in some Middle Eastern countries, such as Egypt or Sudan, as *zar* (which means "visit," because a ghost "visits" a person), meet on special occasions and follow complicated and time-consuming rituals. In traditional families in Egypt, the Sudan, and now also in some countries of the gulf coast, the *zar* cult has healing functions, especially, but not only, for women. This is particularly the case with mental disorders or psychosomatic diseases that are connected with family stress and marital relations or more generally with reactions to unexpected and quick cultural change. Communal meals are eaten as a part of this ritual. This will intensify the personal relations between the participants of the ritual and is part of the payment to the organizers of the ritual. For the ritual meals, coffee beans, nuts, salted and sugared almonds, dates, rice, potatoes, flour, cheese, olives, various sweets, butterfat from the buffalo, meat, tea, onions, tomatoes, spinach, and garlic, among other things, are needed. The quantities depend on the number of participants and the fame of the organizing group and its (female) leader. Initiates will receive special food after their first participation. This may be sugar, bread, or salt. On the seventh day after the ritual, another meal is prepared for them consisting mostly of milk rice and peas and perhaps a chicken or any other bird.[7]

There are no clear-cut divisions between healing practices and humoral medicine and a kind of modern folk medicine that is also called prophetic medicine. But while humoral medicine is a type of traditional medicine that has some claim to modern science and is practiced by professionals, modern folk medicine is a healing technique that is used by non-specialists. Nevertheless, there are many books on this kind of medicine printed in huge quantity and obviously addressed to the uneducated. The authors are sometimes amateurs in the health field. Typically for this kind of folk medicine, no explanations are given as to why certain illnesses arise in certain people and not in others, and only rarely is it explained why suggested therapies have an effect. Most of the suggestions for healing have something to do with food and eating. First, they try to improve the general health of the people through some dietary rules. One of the often-repeated rules is that one should not drink too much water, especially during a meal, because the water will impede the blood circulation. People are also advised to drink a small quantity of cider vinegar before or after a meal. Perhaps this has to do with the Muslim taboo on wine, but in modern Western folk medicine, cider vinegar also plays an important role. It can be taken straight, or as a teaspoonful mixed with water in a glass. It is repeatedly stressed that this practice will strengthen the constitution. The intake is increased with certain maladies.

The other often-recommended food is honey. One author called it a complete pharmacy.[8] Some recommend honey to be substituted for white sugar, because it is said to be more healthy. Honey is also indicated as a major nutrient for children. A child should have at least one spoonful of honey every day. This will make a child strong. Honey is also thought to be a very good remedy for many maladies. For example, honey is used as a remedy for coughing. One of the recipes goes like this: A lemon is cooked in water on medium heat for about 10 minutes. The lemon is then cut in half, and the juice is pressed out into a cup. Two spoonfuls of glycerin are mixed with the juice. The rest of the cup is filled with honey, and the mixture is applied to the patient.

If honey and cider vinegar are so extraordinary healthy, then it does not come as a surprise that the combination doubles their positive effects. Mixtures of honey and vinegar are said to be effective against insomnia or trouble falling asleep. People are advised to always have a cup of that mixture at their bedside and to drink a sip or two before lying down, and to repeat this procedure if sleep does not come shortly. It is also said that the frequent drinking of mixtures of honey and vinegar can help lower blood pressure. Honey is also applied externally to help the skin.

People are strongly advised to eat an apple in the evening before sleeping, because that will be beneficial to the teeth, and one will keep healthy teeth until the age of 60 or 70. Other recommended foodstuffs are onions and garlic. A clove of garlic, if pressed over the tooth, will lessen a toothache. Onions and watercress are used as remedies against baldness.

A central thrust of modern folk medicine concerns the health of infants and children. Lots of advice is given peri- and postnatal to mothers. For example, pregnant women should eat dark or brown bread instead of white. They should avoid milk but can eat cheese. Among the different kinds of meat, the organs of the heart, liver, and kidney are preferable, some say, at least once a week. Pregnant women should avoid veal; sheep; and, of course, pork. Fish, seafood, and poultry are better. They should eat honey instead of sugar and a raw egg every day. It is better to eat sweeter things and to avoid the sour. Instead of lemons, oranges, or grapefruit, one should eat apples, grapes, or strawberries.

For babies, the best food is breast milk. Normally infants are breast-fed for eight months. In Islamic law, a child has the legal right to receive the milk of his or her mother until the age of two years. If a marriage fails during that period, the child must stay with the mother, while the father has to pay the mother for feeding, if she does so. If the mother does not have enough milk, other kinds of food should be fed as soon as possible. Especially healthful food is thought to contain milk and honey; egg yolk; and, in Turkey, *pekmez*, which is a thick, dark syrup made from the juice of grapes, pomegranates, or dates. The grape and date syrups are also used to sweeten dishes, unsweetened milk, or wheat-flour puddings. *Pekmez* made from pomegranates is more sour, so children may not prefer it.[9]

MODERN MEDICINE AND NUTRITION

Generally, one could say that Near and Middle Eastern and North African cooking and nutrition are healthy. As in other Mediterranean gastronomies, meat is rare and vegetables often used. The religious purity rules also have consequences for the kitchen, which is important for the health of the people. Of course, in hot regions of the Near and Middle East and North Africa or in summer periods, there is always the risk that food will be spoiled. Traditional households have their techniques to keep food fresh or preserve it. Refrigerators and deep freezers also help to preserve food. Even modern cookbooks still have information about keeping of fruit or vegetables without refrigeration. For instance, one can buy medium-ripe apples. In a cool and dark place, they are said to keep longer.

Nevertheless, stomach and intestinal problems are frequent in the Near and Middle East and North Africa. There are many remedies for dealing with sudden diarrhea, which is nearly unavoidable there because of the climate. Of course, many kinds of medicine are used, but generally every family in the Near and Middle East and North Africa has their own technique. One tradition is to take black tea without sugar and white bread while the problem is acute. Others combine black tea with salted bread sticks, which replenish salt. For many natives as well as foreigners, a sip of a strong liquor such as whiskey, cognac, or a local brand such as *raki* is considered to be the best remedy. In Lebanon and in other countries where apples grow, the tradition is to rub apples on the skin. These mashed apples are also said to be a good remedy against other stomach and intestinal problems.

As many of the traditional ways of cooking are not passed down to the younger generation anymore, the same can be said about the medical and dietary aspects of food. For a time in the 1970s, information on that aspect of cooking was also missing in cookbooks. This has changed now, as the publishers respond to the increasing demand of the public for health information. Today many of the cookbooks have long sections concerning the most effective washing of all kinds of foodstuffs. It is discussed when to do the washing and how. For example, cookbooks advise the cook not to skin zucchini, because the skin has many important vitamins and so on. One can also find long lists of ingredients and nutritional analysis, as well as medical risks or calories. TV cooking shows only briefly discuss questions of nutrition and health.

Since the 1970s, consumption habits in the Near and Middle East and North Africa have changed. With a growing income, especially in rich oil countries, the quantity and quality of consumed food has increased. This means that more meat is now on the table and more sweets are consumed. This has meant an increase in body weight of men, women, and even children, particularly in the middle class. Consequently, weight loss in now being discussed. Various diet programs have been imported from the West. Between Casablanca and Tehran, everything has been tried, from the Mayo diet to Atkins and Weight Watchers, with as much success as between New York and San Francisco or London and Moscow. No diet program that has been developed in the region has been accepted by the public. Since the early 1990s, there has been a growing market for fitness studios. In Muslim countries where the gender segregation is more strict, some studios are reserved for women only, and others have special hours for them.

Women are generally much more interested in the practical side of the health of their families. Housewives react to health problems in their families with a change in diet (or at least a change in spicing) for their family members. So, in some cases, they avoid hot spices, or reduce fat. In many cases they act according to old rules that they have learned from their mothers, according to their experience, or after consultation with a medical doctor. Health and nutrition are a popular subject not only in female private circles (particularly middle-class women), but also in newspapers and electronic media. One can find health features in newspapers in different sections such as sciences, or sports, but very often in pages dedicated to women. In new magazines that specialize in cooking, health and healthy-cooking topics play an important role. Some issues focus on health food or on losing weight, or recipes will have health and nutrition information. Some magazines are devoted solely to health food.

NOTES

1. Reinhold Loeffler, *Islam in Practice: Religious Beliefs in a Persian Village* (New York: State University of New York Press, 1988), 159.

2 Loeffler, *Islam in Practice*, 125.

3. Bess Donaldson, *The Wild Rue* (New York: Arno Press, 1938), 124.

4. Donaldson, *Wild Rue*, 193.

5. Donaldson, *Wild Rue*, 191–92.

6. Rudolf Kriss and Hubert Kriss-Heinricht, *Volksglaube im Bereich des Islams* (Wiesbaden: Harrassowitz, 1962), 21–22, 25–26.

7. Kriss and Kriss-Heinricht, *Volksglaube im Bereich des Islams*, 179.

8. Muhammad Ali Qurni, *Sihatuka fi al-tabi'a wa-l-a'sha* (Cairo: al-Markaz al-Arabi al-hadith, 1983), 8–9.

9. Marie-Hélène Sauner-Nebioglu, *Evolution des pratiques alimentaires en Turquie: Analyse comparative* (Berlin: Klaus Schwarz Verlag, 1995), 311–12.

Glossary

arrak   Strong alcoholic drink, like pastis, that turns white when mixed with water.

Ashura   10th day of the Muslim month of Muharram, first month of the Muslim calendar.

ayran   Turkish salted yogurt drink.

bedouins   Arab nomads of the Arabian peninsula and the Fertile Crescent.

boza   Beerlike alcoholic drink, especially in Egypt.

brik   North African bread filled with meat, eggs, or vegetables, made from thin leaves of wheat dough.

bstilla   Dish with cooked fowl, fish, or vegetable, wrapped in special layers of thin wheat dough, from North Africa.

burgul/bulgur   Partially cooked cracked wheat.

caliphate   Monarchical Muslim states, especially during the Middle Ages.

chermoula   Thick, spicy mixture of garlic, salt, parsley, cilantro, pepper, lemon juice, vinegar, and oil, from North Africa.

döner-kebab   Slices of spiced or marinated meat grilled on a spit in an upright position from one side, continuously turning around (*döner* is Turkish for "turn around").

fazanjun   Dish of wild ducks cooked in pomegranate juice, from Iraq and Iran.

Fertile Crescent   Geographical designation for the Middle Eastern countries of Israel and Palestine, Syria, Lebanon, and Turkey.

ful mudammas   Dish made of beans (*vicia faba*), onions, tomatoes, garlic, and spices.

haram   Complex term meaning "holy," "forbidden," or "not ritually clean."

harira   Soup made of chickpeas, lentils, onions, tomatoes, and so on, traditionally eaten for breaking the fast during Ramadan, from North Africa.

harisa   Hot, thick chili sauce from North Africa.

hummus   Chickpeas, but also chickpea dip with tahini.

Id   Muslim religious feast.

Iftar   Breaking of the fast during Ramadan.

mawlid   Feast in commemoration of the birthday of a Muslim saint.

mezze   Combination of various hot and cold hors d'oeuvres, including up to 40 different dishes.

muezzin   Caller for the ritual Muslim prayer.

muhallabiya   Middle Eastern milk pudding.

Muharram   First month of the Muslim calendar.

qanun   Portable stove, made of clay or iron.

raki   See **arrak**.

Ramadan   Muslim month of fasting (ninth month of the Muslim lunar calendar).

Shia/Shiite   Minority branch of Muslims.

Sunna/Sunni   Majority branch of Muslims.

tahini   Sesame paste, used in the famous hummus dip.

tajine   Typical North African dish, consisting of a plate and a conical lid; also the name of the dishes cooked in it.

zar   Obsession cult, especially in Egypt and Sudan.

za'tar   Dry spice mixture made mostly of thyme and wild marjoram, sesame seeds, and sumac.

Selected Bibliography

Al Hashimi, Miriam. *Traditional Arabic Cooking*. Reading, UK: Garnet Publishing, 1993.

Allen, Tony. "Food Production in the Middle East." In *Culinary Cultures of the Middle East*, ed. Sami Zubaida and Richard Tapper, 19–31. London: Tauris, 1994.

Arberry, A. J. *The Seven Odes: The First Chapter in Arabic Literature*. London: Macmillan, 1957.

Basan, Ghillie. *Classical Turkish Cookery*. London: Tauris, 1997.

Chase, Holly. "The Meyhane or McDonald's? Changes in Eating Habits and the Evolution of Fast Food in Istanbul." In *Culinary Cultures of the Middle East*, ed. Sami Zubaida and Richard Tapper, 73–85. London: Tauris, 1994.

Donaldson, Bess. *The Wild Rue*. New York: Arno Press, 1938.

Douglas, Mary. *Purity and Danger: An Analysis of Concepts of Pollution and Taboo*. London: Routledge and Kegan Paul, 1966.

Fadel, Maria. *Damaskus. Der Geschmack einer Stadt, aufgezeichnet von Rafik Schami*. Zürich: Sanssouci, 2002.

Firth, Raymond. "Cooking in a Kelantan Fishing Village." In *The Anthropologist Cookbook*, ed. J. Kuper, 182–88. London: Macmillan, 1967.

Fragner, Bert. "Social Reality and Culinary Fiction: The Perspective of Cookbooks from Iran and Central Asia." In *Culinary Cultures of the Middle East*, ed. Sami Zubaida and Richard Tapper, 63–71. London: Tauris, 1994.

———. "Zur Erforschung der kulinarischen Kultur Irans." *Die Welt des Islams*, vols. 23, 24 (1984): 320–60.

Goody, Jack. *Cooking, Cuisine, and Class: A Study in Comparative Sociology*. Cambridge: Cambridge University Press, 1982.

Granqvist, Hilma. *Muslim Death and Burial: Arab Customs and Traditions Studied in a Jordanian Village*. Helsingfors: Soderstorm, 1965.

Grotzfeld, Heinz. *Das Bad im arabisch-islamischen Mittelalter*. Wiesbaden: Harrassowitz, 1970.

Guinaudeau-Franc, Zette. *Les secrets des cuisines en terre Marocaine*. Paris: Sochepress, 1981.

Harrer, Gudrun. "Die fetten Katzen von Baghdad." *Häuptling eigener Herd* 18 (2004): 29–34.

Harris, Marvin. *Good to Eat: Riddles of Food and Culture*. New York: Simon and Schuster, 1985.

Hattox, Richard. *Coffee and Coffeehouses: The Origins of a Social Beverage in the Near East*. Seattle: University of Washington Press, 1985.

Heine, Peter. "Kochen im Exil—Zur Geschichte der arabischen Küche." *Zeitschrift der Deutschen Morgenländischen Gesellschaft* 139 (1988): 318–27.

———. "The Revival of Traditional Cooking in Modern Arab Cookbooks." In *Culinary Cultures of the Middle East*, ed. Sami Zubaida and Richard Tapper, 143–52. London: Tauris, 1994.

———. *Weinstudien: Untersuchungen zu Anbau, Produktion und Konsum des Weins im arabisch-islamischen Mittelalter*. Wiesbaden: Harrassowitz, 1982.

Heine, Peter, et al. "Ful Medames." *Petits Propos Culinaires* 43 (1993): 47.

Kriss, Rudolf, and Hubert Kriss-Heinricht. *Volksglaube im Bereich des Islam. Vo. 2 Amulette, Zauberformeln und Beschwörungen*. Wiesbaden: Harrassowitz, 1962.

Lane, Edward. *An Account of the Manners and Customs of the Modern Egyptians: Written in Egypt during the Years 1833–1835*. London: East-West Publications, 1978.

Lewicki, Tadeusz. *West African Food in the Middle Ages*. Cambridge: Cambridge University Press, 1974.

Loeffler, Reinhold. *Islam in Practice: Religious Beliefs in a Persian Village*. New York: State University of New York Press, 1988.

Love, John F. *McDonald's: Behind the Arches*. New York: Bantam Books, 1995.

Mausili, Zubaida. *Min alfann al-tabkh al-Sa'udi*. Jiddah: Dar al-'ilm, 1990.

Mintz, Sidney W. *Sweetness and Power*. New York: Viking and Penguin, 1985.

Ricard, Paul. "Gateaux Berères." *Hespéris* 6 (1926): 426–29.

Roden, Claudia. *A Book of Middle Eastern Food*. London: Thomas Nelson, 1968.

———. "Jewish Food in the Middle East." In *Culinary Cultures of the Middle East*, ed. Sami Zubaida and Richard Tapper, 153–58. London: Tauris, 1994.

Sauner-Nebioglu, Marie-Hélène. *Evolution des pratiques alimentaires en Turquie: Analyse comparative*. Berlin: Klaus Schwarz Verlag, 1995.

Schopen, Armin. *Geschichte und Gebrauch des Genussmittels Catha Edulis Forsk. in der Arabischen Republik Jemen*. Wiesbaden: Franz Steiner Verlag, 1978.

Seidel-Pielen, Eberhard. *Aufgespiesst. Wie der Döner über die Deutschen kam*. Berlin: Rotbuch, 1996.

Touitou, Odette. *Tunisie—La cuisine de ma mère*. Geneve: Edition Minerva, 2003.

Watson, Andrew M. *Agricultural Innovation in the Early Islamic World: The Diffusion of Crops and Farming Techniques, 700–1100*. Cambridge: Cambridge University Press, 1983.

Zubaida, Sami. "National, Communal, and Global Dimensions in Middle Eastern Food Cultures." In *Culinary Cultures of the Middle East*, ed. Sami Zubaida and Richard Tapper, 33–45. London: Tauris, 1994.

WEB SITES

http://www.jewish-food.org
http://www.globalgourmet.com
http://www.middleeastnews.com

Index

About the Author

PETER HEINE is a Middle East specialist who has written frequently on Arabic cuisine.

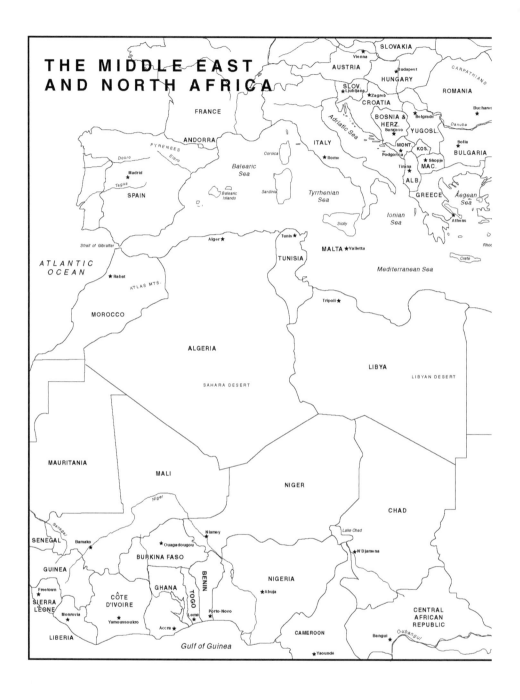

THE MIDDLE EAST
AND NORTH AFRICA

SLOVAKIA
Vienna
AUSTRIA   Budapest
                 HUNGARY   CARPATHIANS
SLOV.
Ljubljana Zagreb   ROMANIA
CROATIA
FRANCE   Bucharest
           BOSNIA &
           HERZ.   Belgrade
           Sarajevo YUGOSL.   Danube
ANDORRA   ITALY   MONT.   KOS.   Sofia
PYRENEES   Podgorica   BULGARIA
Douro   Corsica   Tirana   Skopje
                                          MAC.
Ebro   Balearic   ALB.
           Sea   GREECE   Aegean
Madrid   Rome   Sea
Tagus   Balearic   Tyrrhenian
           Balearic   Islands   Sea   Ionian   Athens
SPAIN   Sardinia   Sea
                                                             Rhod
Strait of Gibraltar   Alger   Tunis   Crete
ATLANTIC   Tunis   MALTA Valletta
OCEAN   TUNISIA   Mediterranean Sea
           Rabat
           ATLAS MTS.   Tripoli

MOROCCO   LIBYA
                                                 LIBYAN DESERT
           ALGERIA

                    SAHARA DESERT

MAURITANIA
                    MALI
                                       NIGER
                    Niger   CHAD
           Niger
SENEGAL   Niamey   Lake Chad
        Bamako   Ouagadougou
GUINEA   BURKINA FASO   N'Djamena
Freetown   B
SIERRA   CÔTE   GHANA E NIGERIA
LEONE   D'IVOIRE   N T   Abuja
      Monrovia   I O   CENTRAL
         Yamoussoukro N G   AFRICAN
           Accra Lomé   Porto-Novo   REPUBLIC
LIBERIA   CAMEROON   Bangui Oubangui
           Gulf of Guinea   Yaoundé

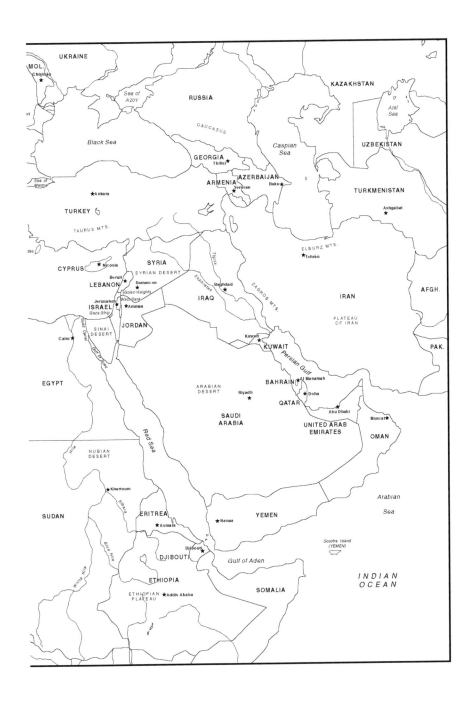